365

Panchatantra

Stories

Published by

An imprint of Om Books International

Corporate & Editorial Office
A 12, Sector 64, Noida 201 301
Uttar Pradesh, India
Phone: +91 120 477 4100

Sales Office
4379/4B, Prakash House, Ansari Road
Darya Ganj, New Delhi 110 002, India
Phone: +91 11 2326 3363, 2326 5303
Fax: +91 11 2327 8091

Email: sales@ombooks.com
Website: www.ombooks.com

Cover: Ratnakar Singh, Sudhir
Illustration: Mukesh, Adil, Kushiram, Rishi
Design: Rajiv Kumar, Rajkumar

ISBN: 978-93-80069-62-3

Printed in Singapore

10 9 8 7 6 5 4 3 2 1

365

Panchatantra
Stories

An imprint of Om Books International

www.ombooks.com

contents

OCTOBER

NOVEMBER

DECEMBER

1 The Blind Vulture

There was once a tree which was home to many birds. One day, a blind old vulture came to live in a hole in that tree. The birds welcomed him and decided to give him a share of their food since he was old. The blind vulture decided to protect their little babies in return. So, they lived happily. One day, a cat passing by that tree heard the baby birds chirping happily. But, as soon as they saw the cat, they began to cry with fright! The blind vulture shouted at once, "Who is there?" Now, the clever cat knew the only way she could eat these tasty tiny birds was if she became good friends with the vulture. She said to him, "I have heard much about your intelligence from the birds on the banks of the river that I just had to come and meet you, Sir." The vulture felt very good when someone praised him. He asked, "Who are you?" She said, "I am a cat." The vulture shouted, "Go away otherwise I'll eat you up." But the smart cat had a good plan. "I live on the

other side of the river. I don't eat meat and take bath everyday in the river," she said. "And I don't think a wise one like you would eat a guest."

The old vulture replied, "How can I trust you, you eat birds!"

"Oh not anymore, Sir!" said the cat. "God punishes those who kill others. I would never kill for food when there are such tasty fruits and herbs to eat in the forest."

The vulture believed her and allowed her to stay with him in the tree hole. Now, everyday the bad cat would eat one baby bird and the blind vulture didn't even come to know. Soon the older birds found that their children were missing! They began to look for them, and as soon as the cat came to know of this, she left the tree and disappeared into the forest. When the birds came to the old vulture to question him, they found him sleeping. And what did they find there? A huge pile of bones! The cat would eat the baby birds and leave the bones in the vulture's tree hole.

All the parents were very angry at the vulture. They thought he had fooled them and broken their trust. Now their poor babies were dead! They cried and shouted in anger and attacked the sleeping vulture. The poor thing didn't even know why the birds were pecking at him and hurting him so painfully.

Finally, he was thrown out with no home and no friends.

2 The King Elephant and the Wise Hare

A long time ago, the great king of elephants ruled over the forest. During his rule once, all the lakes became dry as there was no rainfall. So, all the elephants came to the king for help. They would all die without water! The elephant king said, "Please don't worry! I am your king and so it is my duty to take care of all your needs. You will never again have to live without water. I know of a hidden lake that is always full of water. Let's go there."

While the elephants marched towards the lake, they trampled upon hundreds of hares that had been living there for years. Hundreds of them died and thousands were injured.

The hares were worried. One of them said, "Elephants are so huge and heavy, we are like tiny ants to them. They will continue to trample us every day while going to the lake for water as they can't even see us! If we don't do something quickly we will all be killed. We have to find a way to stop them from coming to the lake. The problem is they are very thirsty and they will never listen to our request."

A smart hare came up with a clever plan and that night he went to the elephant king. He had to be very careful, for if the king became angry they could all be killed! So he bowed down to the king with great respect and said, "The Moon God has sent me, Your Majesty. This lake belongs to him and he has forbidden all of you from drinking water from it."

"But where is your lord, the Moon?" asked the surprised king.

The hare took the elephant king to the lake, and showing the reflection of the moon in the lake, said, "Here he is, the Moon God! Can you see him?"

The elephant king looked down in the lake and replied humbly, "Yes, I can see."

"Move quietly and salute him. Otherwise, he may get very angry and great harm could come to you and your subjects," said the hare.

Believing the hare, the elephant king saluted the reflection and left quietly. The elephants never came back to the lake again and the hares lived happily in their homes.

3 The King Cobra and the Ants

Long ago, a huge king cobra lived in a dense forest. He hunted during the nights and slept during the day. As time passed, he grew so fat that it became difficult for him to squeeze into and out of his hole in the tree. So, he went in search of another tree.

Finally, the cobra selected a very big tree as his new home, but there was a large anthill at the foot of the tree. He slithered up to the anthill angrily, spread his hood and said very rudely to the ants, "I am the king of this forest. I don't want any of you around. I order all of you to find some other place to live. Otherwise, be prepared for your end!"

The ants were so united that they were not scared of the cobra. Instead, thousands of ants marched out of the anthill and soon covered the cobra's whole body with stings and bites! The evil snake slithered away, crying with pain.

4 The Disobedient Kid

A goat and her naughty kid lived together. One morning, the kid went skipping and hopping towards the jungle. The mother goat tried to stop her kid from going alone into the deep, dark jungle, saying, "There are lots of beasts there. Don't go alone."

"Don't worry, Mother. I won't go too far in," the kid said.

The little, frisky kid was so lost in his games that he did not see how deep into the jungle he had come. Soon it turned dark and he wanted to go home to his mother. But the poor frightened kid could not find his way back! He was lost and he didn't know what to do. He cried for his mother and his cozy, warm home, thinking he should have listened to what his mother said. Then, a wolf arrived there and said, "Aha! I shall feast on delicious kid tonight!"

The wolf seized the kid and gobbled him up. The poor kid paid the price for not listening to his mother.

5 The Talking Cave

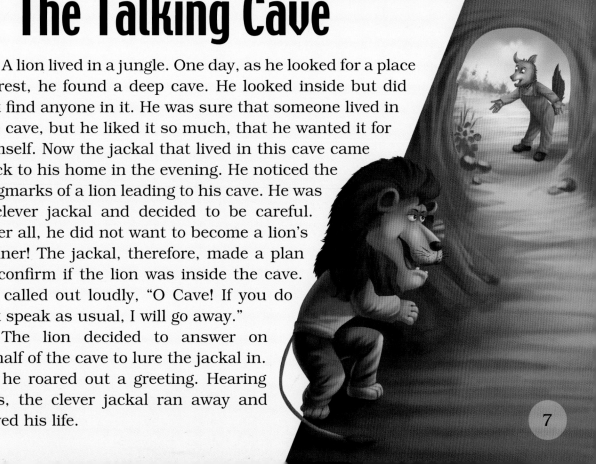

A lion lived in a jungle. One day, as he looked for a place to rest, he found a deep cave. He looked inside but did not find anyone in it. He was sure that someone lived in the cave, but he liked it so much, that he wanted it for himself. Now the jackal that lived in this cave came back to his home in the evening. He noticed the pugmarks of a lion leading to his cave. He was a clever jackal and decided to be careful. After all, he did not want to become a lion's dinner! The jackal, therefore, made a plan to confirm if the lion was inside the cave. He called out loudly, "O Cave! If you do not speak as usual, I will go away."

The lion decided to answer on behalf of the cave to lure the jackal in. So he roared out a greeting. Hearing this, the clever jackal ran away and saved his life.

7

6 The Camel's Revenge

A camel and a jackal, once, became great friends. One day, they went to feast in the watermelon field. After eating, the jackal started howling.

"Please don't howl, your howling will bring the farmer here!" pleaded the camel.

"Singing is good for my digestion," the jackal replied. Soon, the farmer came and beat the camel with a stick, while the jackal ran away.

One day, the camel offered the jackal a ride on his back, while he swam in the river. Once in the river, the camel started to dive under the water. The jackal cried, "What are you doing? I will drown." "I must take a dive if I am in water. Good for my health," said the camel and went under the water leaving the jackal helpless.

7 The False Friend

A deer and a crow were great friends. One day, the crow saw the deer with a jackal. Jackals are known to be cunning animals, so he warned his friend that the jackal could not be trusted.

The deer ignored the crow's warning and went with the jackal to a field where the deer got trapped.

The jackal sneered, "I'm going to call the farmer. He will kill you and I will get a share of your meat."

The deer cried. The crow heard his friend's cries and came to help him. He asked the deer to pretend he was dead.

Soon, the farmer came as he heard the jackal's howls. He saw a deer lying dead in his trap. He opened the trap to check but the deer ran away. The angry farmer hit the jackal and drove him away.

8 The Hen and the Falcon

A falcon and a hen were talking to each other. The falcon said to the hen, "You are the most ungrateful bird." "Why do you say that?" the hen asked angrily. The falcon replied, "Your masters feeds you but you fly from one corner to another, if they come to catch you. You are ungrateful. I am a wild bird yet, I always please those who are kind to me."

The hen asked quietly, "How would you feel if you saw a falcon roasted over a fire? I have seen hundreds of hens being cooked on fire. If you were in my place, you would never come near your masters again and while I only fly from corner to corner, you would fly from hill to hill."

9 The Mouse Turned into a Lion

One day, a sage saw a mouse chased by a cat. The sage with his supernatural powers, made him a cat, to save his life. One day, a dog was chasing this cat. So, the sage turned him into a dog. Another day, the dog was attacked by a lion. The sage immediately made him a lion.

The villagers who knew the lion's secret used to laugh at him. He was just a silly mouse pretending to be a lion! The lion thought he could never stop the jokes until and unless the sage died. So he went to kill the sage.

The sage, seeing the lion coming towards him, knew what was on his mind. And he said, "Go back to your form of a mouse, you are ungrateful and don't deserve to be a powerful lion."

And so the poor lion shrank back into a mouse.

9

10 The Ugly Tree

Once, a long time ago, a forest had straight and beautiful trees. But, in this forest, there was a lonely tree, whose trunk was hunched and bent. The branches were also twisted.

The other trees joked and made fun of this tree, calling it hunchback.

This made the tree very sad. Whenever it looked at the other trees, it sighed, "I wish I was like other beautiful trees. God has been cruel to me."

One day, a wood-cutter came to the forest. He saw the hunchback tree and grumbled, "This twisted tree is useless for me." And then, he cut down all the straight and smooth trees.

Then the hunchback tree realised that God had saved his life by making him a twisted and ugly tree.

11 The Ungrateful Lion

A lion was once caught in a trap cage. He tried all he could to escape, but nothing helped. Then, he saw a man passing by, and asked him to help, promising that he would not eat him. Trusting the lion, the man opened the cage. The lion came out of the cage but forgot all about his promise. He now wanted to eat the man!

The man was worried and thought of a way to save his life. He suggested that they should present their case to a judge. A jackal passing by was asked to be the judge. The jackal was quite clever. He asked them to show him what had actually happened. The lion entered the cage, and as told by the jackal, the man quickly shut the door and locked it! The man and the jackal ran away teaching the ungrateful lion a lesson.

12 The Horse and the Donkey

A washerman had a horse and a donkey. One day, the washer man had loaded his donkey with heavy bundles of clothes. The horse carried nothing.

The load on the donkey was very heavy. So, he requested the horse, "Brother! The load is killing me. Please share some of it."

The horse neighed, "Why should I? We horses are meant for riding."

The donkey kept walking on. Eventually, the donkey fell down exhausted by the heavy load. Then the washer man realized his mistake. He gave water to the donkey and transferred the entire load of clothes onto the horse's back.

The horse repented and thought, "I should have listened to the donkey and accepted half of the load. Now I will have to carry the entire load to the market!"

13 The Dog in a Manger

There was a dog who lived in a barn. He would always sleep on the soft hay, lying in the manger from which the horses ate. The dog's food used to be kept outside the barn in the farmyard, even then the selfish dog would stay right there in the manger. Whenever the horses came in to eat their hay, the dog would start barking at them.

The poor horses could not eat their food! They told the dog that the farmer had left bones for him in the farmyard, but he simply refused to move out of the manger.

"What a selfish dog!" the horses said. "He knows that he cannot eat hay but he will not let us eat our food either. He is ready to trouble himself, just so that he can trouble us!"

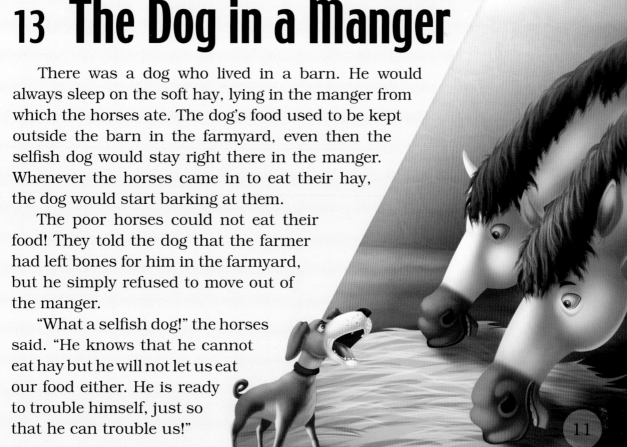

11

14 The Hare and the Tortoise

A proud hare used to make fun of a tortoise. "You move so slowly!" he would say. When the tortoise couldn't bear the daily insults, he challenged the hare to a race.

The hare laughed merrily, "You must be joking! All right, tomorrow morning, we'll go to the other side of the hill and see who reaches first."

The next day, early in the morning, both started the race. The hare raced ahead speedily and decided to rest for a while seeing the tortoise far behind.

Meanwhile, the tortoise continued to move slowly and steadily. By the time the hare woke up, the tortoise had almost reached the finishing line. The hare ran as fast as he could, but the slow tortoise had won the race! The hare realized his mistake. Slow and steady wins the race!

15 The Merchant and the Donkey

A merchant used to visit nearby towns to sell bags of salt, which he used load on his donkey. While on the way to the town one day, the donkey slipped into a pond. The merchant pulled him out. The donkey was suddenly happy. Its load turned very light since almost all the salt had dissolved into the water!

Now, the donkey deliberately slipped in the pond everyday. In time, the master understood the donkey's plan. So, he decided to teach the donkey a lesson.

The next day, the merchant loaded his donkey with cotton bales instead of salt. When the donkey fell into the pond, the cotton bales got wet and became very heavy! The donkey could not even get up now, because of the wight! "Ah! Now you will not try to trick me," laughed the merchant and drove the donkey with his stick.

16 The Story of the Blue Jackal

Once a jackal entered the house of a washer man and hid in a vat full of blue colour used for bleaching clothes. When he came out, he was dyed blue!

When the jackal came back to the forest, all the animals got frightened on seeing such a strange animal. The jackal said, "There is no need to be afraid. I am a special creation of God. He has sent me as your king."

All the animals in the jungle accepted him as their king.

One day, when the blue jackal was holding court, he heard a pack of jackals howling. Thrilled by the sound of his own family, he too began howling loudly like them.

The animals understood that their king was a jackal. So, they beat him hard for fooling them and drove him away.

17 The Wolf and the Crane

One day, a wolf found some bull's meat in the jungle. He started eating the meat greedily. A piece of bone got stuck in his throat. It became difficult for him to even breathe.

Then the wolf remembered that a crane lived nearby. The wolf went to the crane and begged for help and promised a reward in return.

The crane took pity on the wolf and agreed to help. The wolf opened his jaws wide and the crane easily took out the bone. The crane then reminded the wolf of the promised reward.

"What reward?" the wolf remarked. "When your beak was in my mouth I could have just eaten you up! Just be thankful I let you live."

Before the crane could react, the selfish wolf had gone away.

13

18 Two Friends and the Bear

One day, two young friends, Sujal and Piyush, decided to visit a forest. They promised to help each other against any danger. While in the forest, a bear suddenly rushed towards them. Sujal quickly climbed the nearby tree. Piyush, on the other hand, did not have enough time to escape. So he lay down on the ground and acted like he was dead.

The bear growled as it came close to Piyush and appeared to whisper in his ear. Piyush held his breath and kept very still. After sometime, the bear grunted and went away. Sujal came down from the tree and asked Piyush, "What did the bear say to you?"

"The bear told me to stay away from selfish friends who run away at the time of danger," Piyush replied.

19 The True Friend

A long time ago, there lived a pair of parrots on a tree. An old snake also lived in a hole in the same tree. The snake was too weak to go out looking for food. So, the parrots used to leave some food near the hole. The snake was thankful to the parrots.

One day, a vulture hovered over the tree to hunt parrots. Just then, a hunter also came there. He aimed at one of the parrots with an arrow.

When the snake noticed his friends were in danger, it bit the foot of the hunter to save his friends. The sudden snake bite spoilt his aim and the arrow struck the vulture hovering above.

The snake had shown he was a true friend by saving their lives.

20 The Clever Fox

A crow sat on the branch of a tree with a piece of bread in his beak. A fox came there and thought of a plan to get the bread from the crow.

He wished the crow a good day. But the crow did not open his mouth since the piece of bread would have fallen down.

The fox then said, "You are looking very charming. You should have been made the king of all birds. Please sing a song in your sweet voice for me."

The flattered crow could not help himself and replied, "Thanks!"

But as soon as he opened his mouth to speak, the piece of bread fell on the ground below. The clever fox immediately picked up the bread and ran away with it.

21 The Singing Donkey

Once upon a time, there was a donkey that was old and weak.

One night, the donkey met a jackal. They became friends and began to wander around together in search of food.

The next night, they went into a garden of cucumbers and ate as much as they could. The practice went on night after night.

One night, the donkey told the jackal, "I feel like singing."

The jackal said, "Please don't sing, the farmer who owns this place will certainly hear your loud and harsh voice, and he will come after us with a stick. Don't forget that we are thieves here."

But the donkey was in no mood to listen to his friend. The jackal, sensing danger, ran out of the garden. The farmer heard the braying donkey and beat him up nicely for stealing his cucumbers!

22 The Bad Company

Once, a farmer was very sad because some mean crows would come and eat up his crops everyday. He tried putting up scarecrows in the field but they would tear the scarecrows apart.

One day, the farmer laid a net trap in the field. He scattered grains over the net. The crows got caught. The trapped crows pleaded for mercy with the farmer but the troubled farmer said, "I won't leave any of you alive." Suddenly the farmer heard a pitiable cry. He looked carefully at his net and found that a pigeon too had got trapped along with the crows.

The farmer said to the pigeon, "What were you doing in the company of these evil crows? Now, you too will die because you kept bad company." And then the crows and the pigeon became dinner for the farmer's hunting dogs. It's true, bad company always brings harm.

23 The Dog Who Went Abroad

There lived a smart dog called Chitranga in a town. One year, a severe famine struck the town and Chitranga could not find anything to eat. So, he ran away to a faraway land. There was no shortage of food in this new land. He wandered into the backyard of a house where he ate to his heart's content.

One day, some of the local dogs spotted him. At once, they recognized that he was a stranger in their land. They attacked him, biting and growling, and he was hurt very badly.

Finally, when he escaped from them, he thought to himself, "I better leave this place. There may be a famine in my own land, but at least the dogs there are of my own kind."

24 The Wicked Mediator

A sparrow made a home in the cavity of a big tree. One day, he left the tree in search of food and did not return for several days.

Meanwhile, a hare came and started living in his home. When the sparrow returned, the hare refused to leave.

The sparrow said, "Let us go to a judge and we will do as he says."

Meanwhile, a wicked cat came to know about it and met the sparrow and the hare. They explained their problem to the cat. The cat replied in a sweet voice, "I am old and cannot see or hear very well. Come closer and narrate your story." When the poor sparrow and hare came within the reach of the cat, she killed both of them and ate them up! If you fight, you become weak and others take advantage of you.

25 The Flea and the Poor Bug

A bug lived in the linen spread over a king's bed. A flea drifted into the bedroom and said to the bug, "I have never tasted royal blood. So, I will share it with you today."

The bug replied, "You will have to wait till I finish my job. After me, you can have your fill." The flea agreed.

Meanwhile, the king entered his bedroom. The impatient flea began feasting on the king's blood even before he went to sleep. Stung by his bite, the king rose from his bed and asked his servants to look for what was in the bed. The king's men examined the bed closely. The flea sneaked into a dark corner of the bed. The servants found the poor bug and killed him.

26 The Foolish Cats

Once, a cat saw a piece of bread on the road. Another cat saw it too and both pounced upon it at the same time. The cats started fighting.

After sometime, the first cat suggested that they could divide the bread into two pieces. Meanwhile, a monkey came there. The cats asked the monkey to divide the bread into two equal halves.

The monkey was very cunning. He made two pieces of the bread and then he checked their size. Finding one bigger than the other, he ate a bit from the bigger piece. Then he noticed that the other piece was bigger and ate a bit from that.

He carried on like this for some time and at last, he ate up both the pieces, leaving the cats with nothing.

27 The Greedy Jackal

A hunter in the jungle aimed a sharp arrow at a well-fed boar. Though badly hurt, the boar made a wild charge at the hunter putting him to death. The boar too died later from the wounds.

Sometime later, a hungry jackal arrived at the spot where the bodies of the hunter and the boar lay. He said to himself, "God has favoured me today. It will be better, if I begin my meal by eating the gut of this bow."

The jackal went close to the body of the hunter and began nibbling at the gut of the bow. But the gut suddenly snapped with great force, striking and killing the jackal instantly.

He should have had the sense to eat the food, instead he was greedy and came to his end.

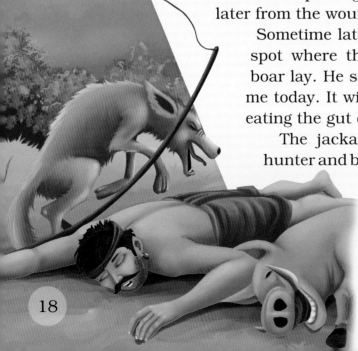

28 The Tale of the Three Fish

Three fish, who were friends lived in a pond. One day, some fishermen passing by the pond wondered, "This pond seems to be full of fish. Let us come at dawn tomorrow and catch some of them."

Overhearing them, the wisest one of the three fish called a meeting and said, "We must move out of this pond tonight."

The second fish also agreed. Laughing loudly, the third fish said, "Why should we leave this pond, the ancient home of our forefathers? We cannot escape death even if we go elsewhere."

Unable to convince him, the other two fish left the pond. The next day, the fishermen took a big catch of fish in the pond. The third fish was one among them.

29 The Curious Monkey and the Wedge

A merchant once began to build a temple and hired workers. One day, when the workers left for lunch, a group of monkeys landed at the temple site.

They began playing with everything that they saw. One of the monkeys saw a partly sawed log of wood lying in a corner. It had a wedge fixed in its centre, so that it did not close up. Curious to know what the wedge was meant for, the monkey began furiously tugging at the wedge.

He heaved and tugged at it with all his might. At last the wedge came off, but not before trapping the legs of the monkey into the rift of the log. The monkey could never extricate his legs out of the closed wood. Finally, the trapped monkey was caught and beaten by the workers.

It is not wise to poke our nose into affairs that are not our concern.

30 The Vain Crows

A poor little mynah lost the way to her nest as it was getting dark. So, she stopped over a tree. There were many crows already perched on this tree, who shouted, "Get off our tree!"

The mynah pleaded, "It might rain. Let me stay for a while." But the crows wouldn't listen.

At last, the mynah flew to another tree where she found a cavity to rest in comfortably. Later, it rained heavily with hailstones falling down. Many crows were hurt and some even died. When the weather calmed down, the mynah came out and flew homewards. One of the crows asked the mynah, "How come you are not hurt?"

"God helps humble creatures and lets arrogant ones like you suffer," the mynah replied.

31 The Mongoose and the Brahmin's Son

A brahmin's wife gave birth to a son. The same day, a female mongoose gave birth to a baby and died. The brahmin's wife brought him up as her own child.

One day, the wife was going to the well to fetch some water. The husband left the house too.

Soon, a snake came and slithered towards the baby. Immediately, the mongoose killed the snake. To show his bravery, the mongoose stood outside the house. The Brahmin's wife arrived and saw the mongoose covered with blood; she thought that he had killed her son. She threw the heavy pitcher of water on the mongoose and killed him.

Then she went inside and found her child safe and a snake, torn to pieces, lying nearby. She was very sad and sorry to have killed the faithful mongoose.

1 The Ass Has no Brains

The lion, the king of the forest, had grown old. Being weak, he could not hunt for his food. So, he called the fox and said, "I appoint you as my minister, you must advise me on all the affairs of the forest, and also bring me an animal to eat everyday."

The fox went out. On the way, he met an ass and said, "You are very lucky. Our king, the lion has chosen you to be his chief minister." The ass said, "I am afraid of the lion. He might kill me and eat me up. And I don't think I am really fit to be a minister!"

The clever fox laughed and said, "Oh, you don't know your great qualities! You have a special charm of your own. Our king is dying to meet you. He has chosen you because you are wise, gentle and hard-working. Now, come with me and meet our great king. He will be really happy to see you."

So, the poor ass was convinced and got ready to go along with the fox.

As soon as they entered the cave, the lion pounced on him and killed him instantly. The

lion thanked the clever fox and was happy to get the food.

As the lion sat down to take his meal, the fox said, "Your Majesty, I know you are very hungry and it is time for your dinner, but the king must take a bath before his meal." The lion thought it was a good idea and said, "You are right. I should go and bathe first. You keep a watch on my dinner."

The fox sat down silently to keep a watch on the king's meal. He was very hungry and thought to himself, "I took all the trouble of getting the ass here. It is I who deserve the best portion of the meal." Thus, the fox cut open the head of the ass and ate up the whole brain. When the lion returned and looked at the ass, he felt that something was missing. He found that the head of the ass had been cut open. He inquired from the fox, "Who came here? What happened to the head of the ass?"

The fox pretended to be innocent and reminded the lion, "Your Majesty, you had given the poor ass a powerful blow on the head when you killed him." The lion was satisfied with the answer and sat down to take his meal. Suddenly, he shouted, "What happened to the ass' brain? I wanted to eat the brain first." The fox smilingly replied, "Your Majesty, asses have no brains. If this one had any, he would not have come here to become your meal!"

2 The Scholars and the Lion

In a small town, there once lived four brahmin scholars who were also great friends. Three of the scholars were very well-read, so they were very clever. But the fourth one, while lacking in knowledge, was rich in common sense.

One of the scholars remarked to the others, "If we go to faraway courts of great kings, our wisdom will earn us fame and fortune."

The others immediately agreed. They all set out on their journey. On the way, they came across the skin and bones of a dead lion.

The first scholar said excitedly, "Let's test the power of our knowledge. Let's try and bring this dead lion back to life! I can put together its skeleton perfectly."

"I can fill the skeleton with flesh and blood," boasted the second scholar.

"I can give life into its body so that it becomes a living creature," said the third scholar.

The fourth scholar said nothing about what he could do.

He resigned, shook his head and said, "Very well, you can please yourselves and do as you wish, but please wait till I climb up a tree. All of you are great scholars. I trust your wisdom and knowledge. You have the power to bring a dead beast to life and soon this lion will roar and be alive. However, I am not sure, if you have the power to change the nature of a beast. A lion never eats grass, as a lamb will never eat flesh."

His scholar friends laughed at him. "You seem to be scared for your life. Shame on you! You trust our knowledge, as you admit, but you have no idea, we enjoy complete control and command over the creatures we create. Why should the beast threaten us when we are the ones to bring it to life? Anyways, you are free to hide anywhere you like to and watch us do our magic!"

The fourth friend quickly ran towards a tree and climbed up on it as his friends still laughed at him.

When the third brahmin scholar breathed life into the lion, the great beast stirred and awoke. Then, with a mighty roar, it leapt upon the three scholars and ate them up in minutes. The brahmin on the tree thanked God for giving him the common sense not to mess with God and his creations.

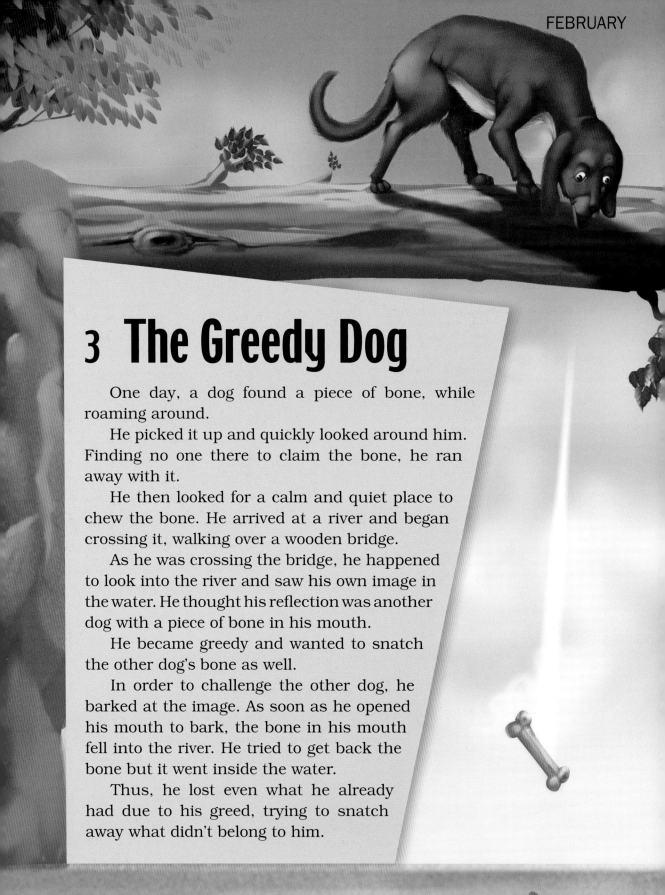

3 The Greedy Dog

One day, a dog found a piece of bone, while roaming around.

He picked it up and quickly looked around him. Finding no one there to claim the bone, he ran away with it.

He then looked for a calm and quiet place to chew the bone. He arrived at a river and began crossing it, walking over a wooden bridge.

As he was crossing the bridge, he happened to look into the river and saw his own image in the water. He thought his reflection was another dog with a piece of bone in his mouth.

He became greedy and wanted to snatch the other dog's bone as well.

In order to challenge the other dog, he barked at the image. As soon as he opened his mouth to bark, the bone in his mouth fell into the river. He tried to get back the bone but it went inside the water.

Thus, he lost even what he already had due to his greed, trying to snatch away what didn't belong to him.

4 The Magic Hen

One day, a poor man came up to a farmer and bought a sack of rice in exchange for a hen.

The farmer's wife was angry when she heard that her husband had parted with a whole sack of rice for an ordinary hen.

But the next morning, the farmer's wife found a golden egg at the place where the hen had roosted during the night.

The magic hen laid one golden egg everyday. This practice went on for several weeks. Soon the farmer became the richest man in the village.

But the farmer's wife, who was a greedy woman, was not satisfied. One day, when the farmer was not at home, she brought a big knife, and cut the hen's belly in the hope of getting all the golden eggs at once. To her dismay, she found that there was not even a single egg inside the hen! And there never would be any more eggs because the foolish, greedy woman had killed the magic hen.

5 The Vain Stag

Once, there was a vain stag. He would often go to a pond to see his reflection and say, "What handsome antlers I have. But I wish I had beautiful legs too."

One day, a lion advanced towards him. He ran into the thick forest but his antlers got caught among the thick bush in the forest. He thought that his end was near, and cursed his antlers for that.

Finally, with the help of his strong legs, he was able to free himself from the branches. Thus, the stag managed to escape from the lion as he darted away on his strong legs.

The stag then thanked his ugly legs that saved his life while his handsome antlers could have been the cause of his death. He thought that he needed his legs more than his antlers to keep him out of danger. Since then, the stag never thought that his legs were ugly.

6 A Bird in Hand

There lived a lion in a forest. One day, the lion sighted a small rabbit playing under a nearby tree. The lion started following him, waiting for a chance to pounce upon the poor little rabbit. When, the rabbit saw the lion, he ran for his life.

But the lion sprang upon him and the little rabbit was in his powerful paws. Before the lion could gobble up the rabbit, a deer came into the lion's view. The greedy lion let the rabbit go and ran after the deer.

The deer leapt away speedily as the lion chased him, and soon disappeared into the forest.

The lion lost the rabbit and failed to hunt the deer as well. He cursed himself for letting the rabbit go away.

It is, therefore, rightly said that a bird in hand is better than two in the bush.

7 The Swans and the Foolish Turtle

Once upon a time, a turtle and two swans were good friends. One year, there were no rains and the pond they used to drink water from, dried up.

The turtle made a plan and told the swans, "Please look for a stick. I will hang on to the centre with my teeth as both of you hold the two sides of the stick and fly with me to another pond."

The swans agreed but warned the turtle, "You have to keep your mouth shut all the time. Otherwise, you will crash to the ground."

The turtle readily agreed. When everything was ready, the swans flew off with the turtle.

On the way, people who saw this sight exclaimed, "Look, how clever the swans are. They are carrying a turtle."

The turtle wanted to respond that it had been his idea, so he opened his mouth to speak and fell to the ground. If only he had forgotten his ego, he would be living safely in the new pond.

8 The Deer Who Played Truant

One day, a doe brought her son to a wise deer and told him, "O learned brother, please teach my little son the tricks to save himself from danger." The teacher agreed. This little deer was very naughty and was interested only in playing with the other deer. Soon, he began missing classes and learnt nothing of self-defence. One day, while playing, he stepped on a snare and got trapped. When this bad news reached his mother, she broke into tears. The teacher went up to her and said softly, "Dear sister, I feel sorry for what has happened to him. I tried my best to teach him self-defence. But he was not willing to learn. A teacher can't do anything if the student is not willing to learn."

9 A Precious Life

The Bodhisattva was once born as a deer. Every animal in the forest admired his handsome looks. One day, a prince came to hunt in the forest.

"This forest is a good hunting ground," remarked the prince.

The prince's eyes fell on the deer and he followed it. He was riding on a horse and started riding fast to catch the deer but the latter ran even faster. Suddenly, his horse fell down and the prince fell into the nearby river. As he didn't know how to swim, the prince shouted for help. The deer heard his cries and dragged him out of the water. Seeing that he was saved by the very deer he had wanted to shoot, the prince felt ashamed and vowed never to hunt animals again.

10 The Greedy Monkey

Once, a monkey had the nasty habit of sneaking into the houses and running away with food. The villagers were highly annoyed with the nuisance of the monkey. They requested a juggler to trap the monkey. He put peanuts in many earthen jars that had very narrow necks and placed them on the rooftops of the houses.

The next day, the juggler saw the monkey on the roof of a house and knew that the naughty monkey would now be easily caught.

When the villagers asked the juggler to reveal the trick, he said that the monkey loved peanuts, so he put his hand into the jar to grab them in his fist. But the neck of the jar was too narrow to allow the clenched fist out. The greedy monkey would not open its fist and let go off the peanuts. Therefore, his hand stayed stuck inside the jar.

The greed caused the monkey's doom.

11 The Jackal and the Drum

Once, a hungry jackal while searching food came to an abandoned field, where he heard strange sounds. The scared jackal instantly wanted to run away in fright.

But after a while he told himself, "Let me find out what the sounds really are and who is making them. I will go and see where this noise is coming from."

Carefully, the jackal tip-toed in the direction of the sounds and found a drum there. "It was this drum that was making the strange sounds whenever the swaying branches of the tree above brushed against it," realized the jackal.

Relieved, the jackal began playing with the drum and thought that there may be food inside it. The jackal entered the drum by piercing its side. He was disappointed to find no food in it. Yet, he consoled himself by saying that he had at least rid himself of the fear of its sound.

12 The Clever Farmer

Once, a farmer had a goat, a bundle of grass and a lion. He had to cross a river on a small boat, which could carry only two of them at a time. The farmer was in a fix. If he takes the lion first, then the goat would eat up the grass in his absence. If he takes the grass, the lion would eat up the goat.

At last, he found the perfect solution.

He first took the goat and left it on the other side of the river. Then he took the lion on his second round. He left the lion and brought the goat back.

Leaving the goat on this side, he took the bundle of grass. He left the grass with the lion and returned to take the goat in the end.

Thus, he crossed the river without any loss.

31

13 The Buck and the Doe

There lived a lovely doe with soft reddish brown fur and wide bright eyes. One day, she was grazing in the forest when a young mountain buck saw her and fell in love with her. He started following the doe day and night. Once he followed the doe to the village despite being warned of the possible dangers. But the love- struck buck didn't pay any heed. After walking a few steps, the doe sensed that a man was hiding ahead. Fearing that there could be a trap nearby she let the buck go first. There was a trap, indeed, and the hunter killed the buck. It was his infatuation that killed him. Infatuation gives one a false feeling of happiness at first but leads to sadness in the end.

14 The Foolish Crane and the Crab

Once, a big banyan tree was home to a number of cranes in a forest. There also lived a cobra in the hollow of that tree. The cobra used to feed on the young cranes. When the mother crane saw the cobra killing her offsprings, she began crying. Her mournful wails attracted a crab, who asked her, what made her cry.

The crane told him everything and requested him to show her some way to get rid of this heartless cobra.

The crab thought to himself, "These cranes are our born enemies. I shall give her an advice that is misleading."

So, the crab advised the crane, "Strew pieces of meat from the mongoose's burrow to the crater of the tree. The mongoose will follow the trail of meat to the cobra and will kill it."

The crane followed the advise. The mongoose came and killed not only the cobra, but also all the cranes on the tree. That is why they say you should never listen to the advice of others unless you know they are your friends.

15 The Donkey and the Washerman

Once, there lived a poor washerman who had a pet donkey. The donkey was very thin because he had very little to eat.

One day, the washerman came across a dead tiger. He thought, "I will put the tiger's skin on the donkey and let him graze in the neighbours' wheat fields at night. The farmers will mistake him for a tiger. The donkey can eat their crops throughout the night, while they would be too terrified to throw him out."

The washerman immediately put his clever plan into action and it worked.

One night, while the donkey was busy eating in the field, he heard a female donkey braying at a distance. He became so excited that he couldn't help braying loudly in return.

Then the farmers came to know the truth and severely beat up the donkey!

It doesn't pay to pretend to be what you are not.

16 The Elephants and the Mice

Once, a group of mice lived in a palace they made, beside a deep lake.

One day, a herd of elephants while going towards the lake, ran over hundreds of little mice.

The mice that survived were worried. The leader of the mice said, "We should appeal to their kindness."

The mice requested the leader of the elephant herd. "Your herd stomped through our home on the way to the lake, killing hundreds of mice. We beg you to take another route."

The elephant leader agreed.

One day, the king ordered to trap all the elephants. The traps were laid in the forest. All the elephants except for one were caught in the traps. Then the elephant that escaped the traps went to the leader of the mice and requested for their help. All the mice hurried towards the trapped elephants and began to chew off the thick ropes with their sharp teeth, freeing all the elephants. Kindness is always returned with more kindness.

17 The Hunter and the Rabbit

Once, a cruel hunter used to catch rabbits and feast upon their meat. One day, he caught a rabbit and started for his home holding him by his ears. On the way home, the hunter met a saint. The saint asked the hunter to free the rabbit and get blessed for the good deed.

The hunter not only refused but decided mercilessly to cut the throat of the rabbit then and there, right before the saint.

He took out a sharp knife from his bag, but when he tried to cut the rabbit's neck, the knife slipped from his hand and fell on his foot, severely injuring him. He instantly cried out in pain and released the rabbit.

The hunter paid the price for his sins. Since his foot was very badly injured, he could not walk properly and became unfit to hunt ever again.

18 How a Sparrow Came to Grief

A female sparrow made a beautiful nest under a big tree. One day, it rained heavily. A monkey completely drenched in the rain and shivering from the cold, came rushing to the tree for cover.

Feeling sorry at the condition of the monkey, the female sparrow said, "You seem to be an able animal. Why didn't you build a house so that you could shelter yourself from the rain and cold?"

Angered by this, the monkey said, "Why don't you shut up and mind your own business?"

The monkey thought to himself, "I must teach her a lesson, if she doesn't stop advising me."

Turning to the female sparrow, the monkey said, "Haven't you heard this saying of the elders that you should only offer advice to those who seek it?"

When the female sparrow persisted with her advice, the monkey climbed up the tree and tore away her nest.

19 The Crow and the Oyster

One day, a hungry crow found an oyster on the beach. In order to eat the tasty meat inside, he tried to break open the oyster. The oyster didn't open. He then tried to use his beak to take out the meat, but failed to open the shell. Then he hit the oyster with a stone, but it still remained tightly shut.

Meanwhile, another cunning crow came by and said, "My friend, the oyster will not open the way you are trying," and continued, "I advise that you take the oyster in your beak and fly high into the air, then drop it onto the rocks below. Only then it will break open."

The hungry crow liked the idea and hence followed the suggestion.

The crow flew up with the oyster and it broke open as the crow dropped it from above. But the other crow picked it up and ate the meat inside. By the time the first crow reached there, only the pieces of broken shell were left for him.

20 Coronation of an Owl

When the world was created, all the creatures flocked with their fellow members to choose their respective kings. The human beings chose a gracious deserving young man, the animals chose the mighty lion and the fish chose the large fish named Ananda, as their respective rulers.

Birds also gathered to make a choice of their king. They chose the owl as their king and recited, "Today, at this auspicious hour, we choose owl as our king."

Suddenly, a crow interrupted. "Why should a grumpy owl be a king with so many younger and wiser crows around?" The birds too felt that and therefore, decided to choose swan as their king. Since then, the crow and the owl are at loggerheads.

21 The Greedy Crow

Once, a pigeon made his nest in the basket that used to hang near the window of a merchant's kitchen. The merchant instructed his cook not to shoo away the pigeon.

One day, a crow befriended the pigeon so that he could have a chance to enter the kitchen.

That day, the merchant's cook prepared a delicious dish of fish. When the cook left the kitchen, the crow flew down into the kitchen to eat the delicious fish. But, the plate covering the dish struck the floor with a loud bang.

The noise was heard by the cook and he rushed into the kitchen. By then, the crow had got hold of a piece of fish.

Seeing the fish in the crow's beak, the cook became furious. He ran and caught the crow by the neck and plucked out all the crow's feathers and wings and then threw him out of the window.

22 The Greedy Crane and the Crafty Crab

Once, an old crane found it difficult to find prey because of his old age. So, he made a plan. He stood on the edge of a lake and said, "Astrologers have forecast that it will not rain for twelve years."

Alarmed, everyone from the lake came to the crane and requested his help. The crane said, "There is a big lake nearby. I can ferry all of you one by one to that lake." Everyone agreed to the proposal. Everyday, the crane would take them one by one to a lonely place and eat them. It was a crab's turn to be taken to safety.

As the crane was flying close to the spot where he ate all the fish, the crab saw a heap of fish bones and asked the crane, "I see no lake anywhere. Tell me, where is it?"

"There is no lake. I am going to kill you," said the crane. The brave crab caught the neck of the crane and crushed it to death, saving his own life. The evil crane got his due punishment.

23 The Dove and the Bee

One day, a bee came to a spring in search of water.

It was necessary for the bee to climb onto a blade of grass to reach the spring and drink water. Unfortunately, while climbing the blade of a grass, she fell into the water.

A dove was sitting on a nearby tree. Seeing the bee in trouble, the dove dropped a leaf near the struggling bee. The bee climbed over it. Soon after, the leaf carried her to safety on to the high ground.

As the bee reached the ground, a hunter arrived there. He was about to shoot the dove when the bee noticed what the hunter was up to. She immediately rushed towards the hunter and stung him on the hand. The hunter cried in pain and dropped the gun on to the ground.

Meanwhile, there was enough time for the dove to fly to safety.

24 The Brahmin and the Cobra

Once, a brahmin while working on his land, saw a big cobra.

He brought a bowl of milk and kept it near the anthill. The next day, he found a gold coin in the bowl. This went on as the brahmin started collecting gold coins everyday.

One day, he asked his son to leave a bowl of milk for the cobra. The son did the same. When he was collecting the coin, greed came to his mind and he thought to kill the cobra to collect all the gold at once.

So, he struck the cobra with a big stick. The, cobra slithered away to avoid the blow but bit the boy, who died soon.

The next time, when the brahmin offered milk to the cobra as usual, the serpent just went away. The brahmin realized that once a strong friendship built on trust is broken, it can never be restored.

25 The Crocodile and the Brahmin

Once, a crocodile trapped in slush requested a brahmin to carry him to the river Ganges.

The Brahmin put the crocodile into his bag, and carried him. Just as he was about to release the crocodile into the holy water, the reptile seized him in his huge jaws.

The brahmin cried out, "You want to repay me by eating me!"

"Don't you know that you can eat the person who has sustained you, if your survival depends on it," the crocodile said.

"I think we should consult a judge," the brahmin said. The crocodile agreed.

The brahmin turned to a fox passing by, and requested him to judge their case. The fox said he wanted to see how the two had journeyed together. They came back only to dump the crocodile in the slush from where the brahmin picked him up. The brahmin and the fox ran away leaving the crocodile trapped there.

26 The Selfish Friend

Once, a mouse made its home in the cave of a lion. The mouse used to trouble the lion by frolicking over his body or biting it sometimes. The lion was very annoyed. But, the mouse was too small for the lion to catch.

The lion met a cat and decided to befriend her so that she could help him catch the mouse. He befriended the cat, brought her to his cave and gave her food.

One day, when the lion was out hunting, the mouse dashed out of his hole to look for some food. The cat saw the mouse and instantly killed it.

When the lion returned, the cat informed him that the mouse had been killed.

The lion's behaviour towards the cat suddenly changed. The cat had served the lion's purpose, so the lion stopped feeding her.

The cat realized what a selfish friend the lion had been and left the cave.

27 Grandma's Beloved

There lived an old woman with a black calf whom she loved very dearly. Due to their love, everybody started calling him Grandma's Beloved.

The calf grew up into a strong bull and decided to earn some money for his old mistress. One day, he met a merchant who was stranded on the shore as his bullocks were unable to pull the carts across the river. The merchant told Grandma's Beloved, "If you help in pulling my carts, I promise to give you two gold coins." The bull pulled all his carts across. The merchant put the two gold coins in a small bag and tied it around the bull's neck. Taking his hard-earned money, the bull returned home happily to give his mistress a pleasant surprise.

28 The Farmer and the Cow

Once upon a time, Dharmapal, a farmer, had a cow which gave lots of milk. One day, the cow fell ill and stopped giving milk. The farmer thought that she would not recover and left her out in the forest.

The cow ran away to another village and fell down unconscious outside the house of Madho, a poor farmer. Madho treated her so well that she soon recovered. The cow started giving milk and Madho earned good money by selling the milk.

Soon, the cow's fame spread everywhere. When Dharmapal heard about it, he came to Madho and asked him to return the cow. But Madho refused.

They took the case to the village head. He placed both the farmers on either side of the cow and then left the cow free in between them.

The cow immediately went to stand by the side of Madho. The head of the village decided that the cow belonged to Madho for he had loved and cared for her in her time of need.

1 The Bird Pair and the Sea

There once lived a pair of pheasants close to the sea.

One day, the female pheasant told her husband that she was going to have babies, and he must look for a safe place to lay the eggs. The husband said, "My dear, this seaside is enchanting and it is better you lay eggs here." The wife said, "When it is full moon, the tide of the sea can wash away even wild elephants. Let us go elsewhere." Amused, the husband said, "What you say is true. But the sea has no power to harm us. You can lay your eggs here." Listening to this dialogue, the sea thought, "How vain is this bird, no bigger than a worm! Let me drown these eggs and see what he can do." After laying eggs, the female bird went in search of food. In her absence, the sea sent a wave that sucked the eggs into the waters.

The female returned to the nest and, not finding the eggs there, told the husband, "You are a fool. I told you that the waves would wash away the eggs."

"Don't worry, my dear. I'll think of a way to teach him a lesson. I will siphon off all the water in the sea and leave him dry," said the husband. "But how can you consume all the water in the sea? Call all your friends and try to do the job together," advised the wife. Impressed by his wife's wisdom, the husband agreed. As their friends, the cranes, the peacocks, the cuckoos and other birds, gathered, the male pheasant told them the story of how the sea had killed their offspring and how necessary it was to drain him out. They said, "We cannot do this job. Let us go to Garuda, Lord Vishnu's vehicle, and tell him all that has happened. He will be angry over what the sea has done to his species and will surely take revenge." All the birds went to meet Garuda and told him, "O lord, we need your help. The sea has destroyed the eggs of the pheasant pair." Moved

41

by their sad story, Garuda went to Lord Vishnu and told him everything. "Come with me. I shall recover those eggs from the sea and make the pheasant pair happy again," said Lord Vishnu. The Lord then took out his thunderbolt and aiming it at the sea warned him, "Return the eggs to the bird pair. Otherwise, I will turn you into a desert." Frightened, the sea returned the eggs to the pheasants. The male pheasant handed them to his wife. He who challenges an enemy without knowing his strength perishes in the end.

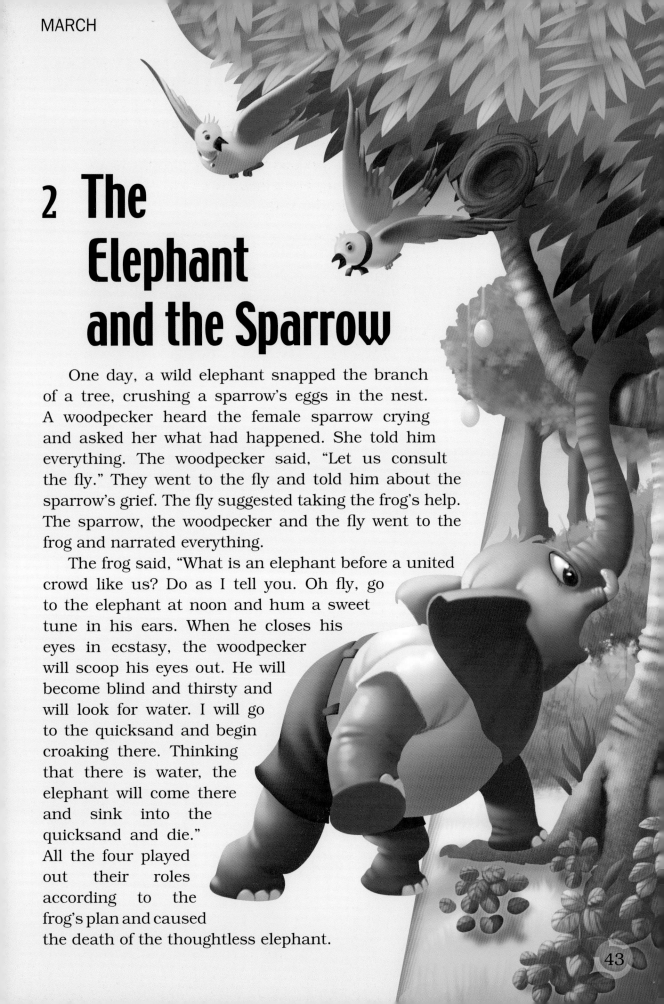

2 The Elephant and the Sparrow

One day, a wild elephant snapped the branch of a tree, crushing a sparrow's eggs in the nest. A woodpecker heard the female sparrow crying and asked her what had happened. She told him everything. The woodpecker said, "Let us consult the fly." They went to the fly and told him about the sparrow's grief. The fly suggested taking the frog's help. The sparrow, the woodpecker and the fly went to the frog and narrated everything.

The frog said, "What is an elephant before a united crowd like us? Do as I tell you. Oh fly, go to the elephant at noon and hum a sweet tune in his ears. When he closes his eyes in ecstasy, the woodpecker will scoop his eyes out. He will become blind and thirsty and will look for water. I will go to the quicksand and begin croaking there. Thinking that there is water, the elephant will come there and sink into the quicksand and die." All the four played out their roles according to the frog's plan and caused the death of the thoughtless elephant.

3 The Foolish Crow

A hawk once lived on the top of a hill. In the valley, a crow had made its nest on a banyan tree. The crow was foolish and lazy and never wanted to work hard at hunting for food. He wished to feed on the rabbits, which lived in a hole under the same tree. The hawk used to hunt the rabbits occasionally by swooping down on them from above.

The crow's mouth watered at the thought of eating tasty rabbit meat. One day, he decided that he must hunt like a hawk in order to catch a rabbit. So the next day, the crow flew very high in the sky and then came down in a fast swoop after spotting a rabbit. But there cannot be a comparison between a hawk and a crow. The rabbit had noticed the crow and hid behind a rock. The crow came down blindly and dashed against the rock and died on the spot.

One must not blindly copy others, but must keep in mind one's own capacity and skills.

4 The Hawk and His Friends

A young hawk lived on a tree by the side of a lake.

One day, he said to a female hawk, "Dear, I want to marry you." The female hawk asked him to first make a friend.

The hawk approached a lion, who agreed to be his friend. Then, the two hawks got married and soon had some babies. Once, two hunters came with the intention of catching the birds living under this tree. The parent hawks got worried about the safety of their babies, and the female hawk sent her husband to seek his friend's help.

The hawk called the lion, who roared loudly. When the hunters saw a huge lion approaching them, they quickly ran away.

Now the hawk understood the value of a friend.

5 The Frogs and the Snake

A snake made a plan to eat all the frogs of a lake. The snake said to the frogs, "I am here to serve you under a brahmin's curse." The frog king was thrilled and narrated this to all the frogs. All the frogs hopped on to the snake's back to take a ride.

The next day, the snake said, "I've had nothing to eat; I'm too weak to crawl swiftly." The frog king said, "You can eat the small frog at the end of your tail" which he did.

Over the next few days, the snake had eaten all the frogs except the frog king himself.

The next time the frog king said, "You may eat the frog at the end of your tail," the snake gulped him down.

6 The Story of the Jealous Cousin

The Buddha's popularity made Devadutta, his cunning first cousin, jealous. First he tried to kill Bimbisara, main supporter of Budha, thinking that if he were dead, Buddha's popularity would lessen. But he failed.

Then, Devadutta even tried to kill the Buddha. Once he hurled a stone at the Buddha from the Gridhrakut Mountain, but, magically, two other stones came in its way and stopped it. Devadutta was dumbfounded. In yet another attempt, Devadutta set loose a rogue elephant at Rajgruhi where the Buddha went for seeking alms.

The elephant created chaos among the people. The Buddha came to the elephant and gently touched the rogue on his forehead. The elephant calmed down instantly. Devadutta was unsuccessful in his attempts. Eventually, people came to know about his evil plans and drove him out of town.

7 The Sheep and the Wolves

A pack of wolves were eyeing a flock of sheep for feast since long. They sent a messenger to the sheep and asked them to dismiss the dogs from their service. "What's the use of keeping the dogs that are noisy and always barking? Think of a day when we build a friendship and stay peacefully. You will no longer need the dogs at your service when we become friends. This is our proposal. Please think about it." The sheep were silly. They immediately dismissed the dogs from the charge. Their flock had no one to protect it now, and they were in great danger. The wolves wasted not a minute to pounce on them and killed them in no time. The sheep suffered because they exchanged friends for foes.

8 Suchimukha and the Monkeys

A gang of monkeys lived on a mountain. When winter arrived, the monkeys piled some red berries and began blowing at them as if they were glowing embers of coal.

Suchimukha—a bird who was watching the monkeys' activities, called out to them. "The red objects that you are blowing on are not embers of coal, but just wild red berries. Don't waste your energy on them? Why don't you look for a shelter in a cave instead?" A monkey retorted, "Why are you meddling in our affairs? Go away and leave us!" But Suchimukha kept prattling on.

Finally the monkeys were so fed up that they caught and soundly beat up the bird.

It's better not to counsel a fool or offer unwanted advice to everyone.

9 The Quarrel of the Bees

During spring, the female bees remain busy building their beehive, while the male bees hardly work. When the female bees would finish building the hive, the male bees would take it over. Once, they quarrelled over this issue. Finally, they decided to seek justice from the wise hornet. The hornet said, "The male and female bees each have to build another hive. The swarm that will do it will be the true owners of the hive." The male bees did not agree with the judgement because they didn't know how to build a hive. The females, however, found it was easy for them to build another hive.

The judge, then pronounced, "It is now clear that the female bees have built the hive. So, the hive belongs to them!"

10 Unity is Strength

Once upon a time, there lived a flock of doves that flew from place to place in search of food, led by their king. One day, they were all trapped in a net. The doves desperately struggled to get out, but it was of no use.

Then the dove king had an idea. He told all the doves to fly up together at once, thus lifting the net along with them. The doves immediately obeyed their king. The hunter looked up in astonishment as he saw his net rise into the air with the flock of doves. The doves flew to the home of a mouse who was a faithful friend of the dove king. Eventually, the mouse chewed the net with his teeth and freed the doves.

11 The Country Mouse and the Town Mouse

Once upon a time, a town mouse went to the countryside to visit his old friend there. The country mouse was a bit coarse and lived on very little, but the town mouse was hearty and plain. The latter said, "You live like a toad in this hole. Please come with me to my town. I'll show you how beautiful and exciting life can be." The country mouse got curious and set out with his friend. They entered a big banquet hall. On reaching there, they started nibbling on exotic foods. But suddenly, some hounds started chasing them. Gradually, when the coast was clear, the country mouse said to the town mouse, "Bye, my friend. I am happy with my crust. I live in peace whereas you are always chased by tension."

12 The Bird with Two Heads

There lived a two-headed bird named Bharunda. One day, he found a golden fruit. One of the two heads started eating the fruit and found it very tasty. The other head said, "Let me also taste the fruit." The first head replied "We've only one stomach, whichever head eats, the fruit will go to the same stomach." Later one day, the other head found a tree bearing poisonous fruits. He took the poisonous fruit and told the first head, "I will eat this poisonous fruit and will take the revenge." The first head yelled, "Please don't eat it. If you eat it, both of us will die." But the other head didn't bother and ate the poisonous fruit. Thus, both of them lost their lives.

13 The Cobra

Once, there lived two crows in a big tree. A cobra, who also lived there, used to eat up all the babies of the crows. The female crow asked her husband to move to some safer place but he said, "We will kill the cobra." His wife asked, "How is that possible?" He explained the plan, "The king's men come at the river bank for a bath and you have to pick up their golden necklace which they leave on the grass with their clothes, before they go to bathe. Drop the necklace in front of the cobra's home. They will discover the cobra and will kill it." The female crow did just as asked. The vile cobra was killed by the royal guards, and the crows were safe.

Thus, sheer wisdom achieves the goal that cannot be achieved through physical power.

14 The Swan and the Owl

Long ago, a swan lived by the side of a lake. An owl joined him there. They lived together happily. When the summer came, the owl thought of returning to his home. He asked the swan to join him. The swan said, "When the river goes dry, I'll come and join you." When the river went dry, the swan flew to the banyan tree where the owl lived. The swan went to sleep early.

Just then, a few travellers came to rest under the tree. Seeing the travellers, the owl hooted sharply. The travellers took it as a bad omen and one of them shot an arrow at the owl. As the owl could see in the dark, he escaped the arrow and flew away. The arrow pierced the swan instead and the poor thing died! It is rightly said, when in a new place, one must always stay alert.

15 The Donkey and the Dog

Once, a washerman had a donkey and a dog. The dog used to guard his master's house and the donkey used to carry stacks of clothes on his back. One night, a thief got into the house. Even after seeing the thief, the dog didn't bark. When the donkey questioned the dog, he answered, "The master doesn't care for me. He doesn't even feed me properly. I won't wake him up." The donkey requested the dog to bark, but the dog didn't listen to the donkey.

Hence, the donkey brayed at the top of his voice which woke up the washerman. The thief quickly ran away from the scene. The washerman could not find anyone. He got furious at the donkey and thrashed the poor donkey with a stick. One must focus on ones own duty, and let others do their own.

16 The Dolphins and the Sprat

The dolphins and the whales were involved in a war with one another. When the battle was at its height, a sprat stepped in and tried to reconcile them. However, the dolphins refused to accept any help from the sprat. Surprised, the sprat wanted to know the reason. To this, one of the dolphins cried out, "Stay away. We'll prefer death in the war to being reconciled by you—a small fish, so much inferior to us!" The sprat felt bad and went away. The dolphins fought on and each of them was fatally wounded. Even when they were dying, there was pride on their faces. Pompous people would accept damage to any extent than avoid harm with help of people from the lower rungs of society.

17 The Snake and the Farmer

A farmer was returning back to his house on a wintry night. On his way, he saw a snake. He was almost dead with the cold. He took pity on the creature, and brought him home. He kept him close to the fireplace for some time and slowly, the warmth made the snake feel better. But on gaining back his health, the snake sprang up and attacked the farmer's wife and children. The farmer heard them cry. He rushed into the room and saw the horrifying scene. His wife and kids had fainted with fright while the snake was sitting there ready to bite! He quickly grabbed an axe and cut the snake into two halves. The snake died immediately. It is true that kindness, shown to ungrateful ones, is often thrown away.

18 The Cock and the Fox

One day two friends, a dog and a cock, set out to travel. In the night, they took rest under a tree. The cock perched on the branch of the tree, while the dog stayed under the same tree.

At day break, the cock gave a loud crow drawing the attention of a wild fox, who planned to make a good meal of it. He said to the cock, "You will be useful to our fellow creatures. Come join us." The cock understood his motive and said, "Well wake my secretary up. He will toll the bell." As the fox tried to wake the dog up, the dog jumped on him and killed him immediately.

Those who lay traps for others are often caught by their own snare.

19 The Wind and the Moon

A lion and a tiger lived together as friends. A monk also lived nearby. One day, the tiger said, "The cold comes when the moon decreases from full to new." The lion responded, "You are stupid, cold comes when the moon increases from new to full."

They decided to consult the monk for the correct answer.

The monk said, "It can be cold in any phase of the moon, from new to full and back to new again. It is the wind that brings the cold, whether from west or north or east. Therefore, both of you are right." The monk also said, "The most important thing is to live without conflict, to remain united." Both of them lived happily thereafter as good friends. Weather comes and goes, but friendship remains.

20 The Lioness

Once upon a time, all the beasts of the forest were in dispute as to who could produce the maximum number of kids at birth. The wolf boasted, "Minimum five." Others went on adding to it. Then they decided to visit the lioness. They challenged her royal status, and asked, "How many do you have at birth? There are many among us who give birth to a number of kids at a time. We are much superior." They asserted.

"Oh! Is it so! It's just one in my case," said the lioness. All the animals laughed a lot and made fun of the lioness. Then the lioness said, "Mind you, my dear fellows, that 'one' is a lion!" No matter how much you have in quantity, don't argue with quality.

21 The Monkey and the Crocodile

Once, a monkey and a crocodile were friends. The crocodile's mother, who relished monkey's heart, asked him to get one. The crocodile said to the monkey, "Fruits on the island are ripe. I can take you there." The monkey's mouth watered. He sprang on the crocodile's back and off they went towards the island. Midway, the crocodile revealed, "My mother wants to eat your heart and I am taking you to her." The monkey kept his cool. "Oh, but I left my heart in the tree. You'll have to take me back to get it," said the quick-witted monkey.

The foolish crocodile started back towards the riverbank. No sooner than he reached there, the monkey jumped onto the shore, and capered up the tree to safety.

22 The Monkeys and the Bell

Once, a group of monkeys found a bell in the jungle. Every night, the monkeys would enjoy the melodious sound of the bell. The villagers were afraid of the sound believing it to be an evil spirit. An intelligent woman in the village went into the forest to find out the truth. She found that a group of monkeys were playing with the bell.

The woman placed some groundnuts and fruits under a tree in the jungle and watched the monkeys from a distance.

The monkeys dropped the bell and ran to pick the eatables. The woman picked up the bell quickly and came back. The villagers praised her for her presence of mind.

One must not be afraid of trifles. Intelligence and courage succeed against all odds.

23 The Oxen and the Butchers

Once, the oxen decided to blot out the race of butchers from the face of the earth. "See, these evil butchers," they said to one another, "are on this earth only to kill us! So let's fight our own battle against them." They were just sharpening their horns when an old ox came forward with a different opinion. "Look friends," he said, "Make sure you are doing the right thing. No doubt, these butchers kill us with skill. But in this battle if we fall into the hands of the more savage, we'll suffer double death. The whole humankind may exist without butchers, but will they stop eating beef? No. So think again before doing this. Do not be in a hurry to exchange one evil for another."

24 The Two Dogs

Once a dog met a gentleman's dog and they planned to visit the kitchen. The strange dog entered the kitchen through the back door and started wagging his tail at the thought of eating some tasty food. The cook saw him suddenly and grabbed him by his legs. He threw him out of the kitchen. The dog fell into the garden and started yelping. He got up and ran out of the garden. While he was running out the gentleman's dog came to him and asked, "Hi friend! How did it taste?" The other one said, "Friend! I drank so much that I feel dizzy now. I can't find the proper way to get into my house." Those who enter through the backdoor, are often showed the window.

25 The Beetle Who Challenged The Elephant

One day, a dung beetle spotted some empty liquor bottles on a table. He flew near the bottles and licked the few remaining drops and got drunk. Then, buzzing merrily, he returned to his heap of dung. An elephant passing by, sniffed the dung and feeling disgusted by the foul smell, moved away. The beetle under the influence of alcohol imagined that the elephant was frightened of him. He called after the elephant and challenged him to a fight.

"Come on, you big fat fool! Let's fight and see who wins today," he shouted at the elephant. The elephant didn't pay any heed, but the excited beetle continued to jeer at him. Finally, the elephant lost his patience and threw some dung and water on the beetle, killing him instantly. Alcohol gives one false ideas about oneself.

26 The Frogs and the Donkey

A donkey was grazing on a muddy meadow. He set his foot on a hedge and killed two or three frogs accidentally. A small frog went to his mother and said, "Mother, it was a big beast that killed the frogs."

The mother asked, "How big was it? Like me?" The kid said, "No. much bigger."

The mother puffed herself big and asked, "This much?" The kid said, "No. Much bigger than you."

The mother puffed with all her might and said, "Now? I think he was that big."

The kid said, "Mother you will burst! Don't try to be bigger now."

His mother, provoked at the statement, kept trying and ended up in bursting with a bang! No creature can become as great as they think.

27 The Cruel Hornbill

A hornbill was the king of birds. But he was unjust and cruel. The birds decided to make the bulbul their king. The owl said, "I have a plan."

According to the plan, the owl and other birds asked the hornbill to break a thick branch. He struck the branch with his strong bill, but there was no damage done to the branch.

Then, the owl pointed to another thick branch and asked the bulbul to break it. To everyone's surprise, the bulbul broke off the thick branch from the tree. Thus she was made the new king.

Actually, the woodpecker had pecked at the branch for a long time. Just when one more blow was needed to fell the branch, the woodpecker had left it for the bulbul.

28 The Jackal and the Sage

Every night, a wicked jackal went to a neighbouring village to steal delicious food items. The villagers were looking for the thief but they were unable to catch him.

One day, when he went to the village, he saw the villagers were still searching for him. After a while, he saw a sage coming his way. In a piteous voice, the wicked animal cried, "Dear good man, I am injured. Please put me in your bag and carry me home."

The holy man happily agreed and did as was asked. When the jackal reached his den, he cried aloud, "Here is the thief the man with the bag!" and slid inside. The villagers took the sage for the thief.

So, don't ever trust anyone blindly.

29 The Birth of a Banyan Tree

Once there were three friends—a crow, a monkey and an elephant. Often, they had disagreements on many issues but failed to reach any conclusion. One day, they were resting under a big banyan tree when the monkey asked, "What was the size of the banyan tree when you first saw it?"

The elephant said, "As a baby, I used to rub my belly against its tender shoots."

"When I was young, I ate some berries and then dropped a few seeds here. This tree grew up from those seeds," the crow said solemnly.

Hearing him, the monkey said, "Friend, the first time I saw this tree it was a seedling. So, from now on, we shall listen to your opinions as you are oldest among us".

30 The Two Calves and the Piglet

One upon a time, a household had two calves and a piglet. Their master treated the piglet too well, feeding him with porridge. But the two calves who toiled very hard in the field got to eat only grass and hay. The younger calf was very envious of the piglet. "Why should he get all the good food to eat when we do all the hard work?" she complained to the elder one. "Oh no," gasped the latter, "Never envy anyone because you don't know what price that creature may have to pay for his well-being." Very soon, the girl of this house was getting married and the piglet was to be killed for meat. It is for this purpose that he was being fed so well.

31 The Monkey and the Snake Charmer

There was once a snake charmer. He owned some snakes and a monkey. He was very mean to his pets. One night, after being spanked by his owner, the monkey ran away. The snake charmer noticed that people were not enjoying his shows without the monkey. So, he went out in search of him and found him sitting on the branches of a tree. "Oh dear pet, I have missed you so much! Let's go back home!" he cried. "Liar, you have come searching for me not out of love but because you've realized that without me your earnings have gone down!" snapped the monkey angrily. The snake charmer had to return home empty-handed, but learnt an important lesson that one must show love and respect to animals as well.

1 The Camel, the Jackal and the Lion

In a forest, there lived a lion served by a leopard, a jackal and a crow. One day, they saw a camel that had lost its way. The lion said: "Tell him he'll be safe here and bring him to me." The three assistants brought the camel to the lion. The lion said to the camel, "You can remain with us without any fear." The camel agreed and stayed on. One day, the lion was badly injured in a battle with an elephant. He became too weak to hunt. So he asked his assistants to go out and look for some animal for his meal. The leopard, the jackal, and the camel looked everywhere for an animal but could not find any. The jackal took the crow aside and said: "We have the camel. Let us kill him and survive."

"How can you even think of that? Don't you know, we cannot kill him because our master has promised him

protection?" questioned the crow. "Leave it to me. I shall convince our master to kill the camel," said the jackal. The jackal went up to the lion and said, "Oh, lord, we could not find a single animal. I humbly suggest that we make a meal of this camel." Annoyed, the lion said, "If you repeat these words, I shall first kill you. I have given him my word." "You are right my lord. But if the camel voluntarily offers himself as food, obliged as he is by your hospitality, then it is no sin to accept the offer." The lion agreed. The jackal told the others, "Friends, our lord is in a pitiable condition. He cannot hunt for himself. We have an opportunity to offer our help to him now. Let us offer our bodies to him." All of them came to the lion with tears in their eyes. "What's the matter?" asked the lion.

"My lord, we searched every inch of the forest. We found nothing. I request the lord to have me for your meal." said the crow. It was now the turn of the jackal to show his loyalty. Addressing the lion, the jackal said, "Lord, I request you to have me for your meal." The leopard intervened and said, "Oh lord, let me give away my life to save your life." All this set the camel thinking, "All these servants of the master have said what they wanted to say. Still, the lion did not kill any one of them. Let me also offer to be his food." The camel, then came forward and requested the lion to have him for his meal. At once, the jackal and the leopard pounced on him and tore him to pieces and all of them had a delicious feast.

2 The Lion and the Clever Rabbit

Once upon a time, a mighty lion lived in a jungle. He roamed about freely, killing every creature that he came across. The animals were sad to see so many of them killed for no use, and so they came to the lion and said, "You are our king. We want to spare you the trouble of hunting for your food, so we would like to send one animal from amongst us everyday to be your meal." The lion agreed and said, "But remember, one animal has to be at my doorway at lunch time every day or I will kill every single one of you."

After this, there was peace in the jungle. One day, a small, skinny rabbit was chosen to provide the lion's meal. He was clever and had made up his mind to save himself. He walked towards the lion's den, thinking of a plan. On the way, he passed a deep old well and seeing his own reflection in the clear water, he had an idea. Meanwhile, the lion had come out of his den and roared angrily when he saw the rabbit.

The rabbit said, "Your Majesty, it's not my fault that I'm late, nor are the other animals to blame. Four rabbits were sent along with me to make up a hearty meal for you. But on our way, a really big and powerful lion stopped us and demanded to know where we were going. When we told him, he was angry, and roared that he was the real king of the jungle, and that you are just an impostor. He pounced on the other four rabbits and said that they would make an excellent meal for him and sent me to you!"

The lion let out a deep roar of rage. "Who is this impostor who dares to challenge my position?" he exclaimed. "Lead me to him at once!"

The rabbit led the lion to the old well. "Look inside," he said, "and you will see the mighty lion yourself." The lion looked over the rim of the well, and as he looked into it, his own reflection stared back at him. Thinking that it was the impostor looking at him, he leapt into the deep well in rage, and drowned instantly. The clever little rabbit was saved.

Sometimes great strength is no match for a clever mind.

3 The Quails and the Hunter

There was once a quail hunter who hunted many quail and there numbers were decreasing. One day, the king quail called for a meeting with all his subjects and said, "Tomorrow, when the hunter comes to catch us, we will all raise our heads in unison and fly away with the net to save our lives." The plan succeeded and the hunter couldn't catch even a single quail the following day. After a few days, the hunter returned. This time when he spread his net, the quails were trapped again. But, as they all got ready to fly, one quail accidentally stepped on the head of another. And both began to fight, forgetting all about the escape! The hunter caught them as they were unable to hold the net aloft for one another. In their hour of need, they all forgot about unity and therefore the hunter was successful in catching them.

4 The Mischievous Monkey

The Bodhisattva was once born as a hermit. Everyday, when he went to the village to seek alms, a monkey would enter his hut, eat all the food and make all sorts of mischief. Once the monkey came to the hermit's hut but found nothing to eat. So, he went to the village to look for the hermit. The villagers had just performed *puja* and were about to offer the *prasad* to the hermit. The monkey stood near the hermit, joining his hands as if he were in deep meditation. The villagers were pleased to see such devotion in a monkey. But the hermit recognised the mischievous monkey and told the villagers how the monkey troubled him every day. The angry villagers chased him away.

5 The Snake and the Hermit

Once upon a time, there was a poisonous snake in a forest. He lived in a lonely corner where nobody dared to go. One day, a sage came to meditate there.

The hermit asked the snake to leave his evil ways, and stop biting. He then destroyed the poison of the snake with his supernatural powers. The snake followed what the hermit had said to him. After sometime, the hermit left the forest. When he returned, he found the snake half-dead. Being worried, the sage asked him the reason.

The snake said, "As I stopped attacking men, they were no longer afraid of me, and started stoning me. Moreover, I did not get food, so I'm weak."

To this the hermit said, "You should protect yourself from those who harm you. And take natural food." The snake followed it, and lived a better life.

6 How the Monkey Saved His Troop

A troop of monkeys used to eat the ripe mangoes of a tree on the riverbank. One day, the king went fishing to the river. He saw a tree of ripe mangoes. On going close, he found, monkeys were eating mangoes. The king ordered his archers to shoot the monkeys. The chief of the monkeys heard the king's order and immediately thought of a way to save his troop and himself. He climbed up to a branch that hung over the water, walked to the tip of the branch and had every member of his troop jump off his back, one by one, to the hill across the river. All the monkeys reached their home in the hill safely. That is how the monkey saved his troop.

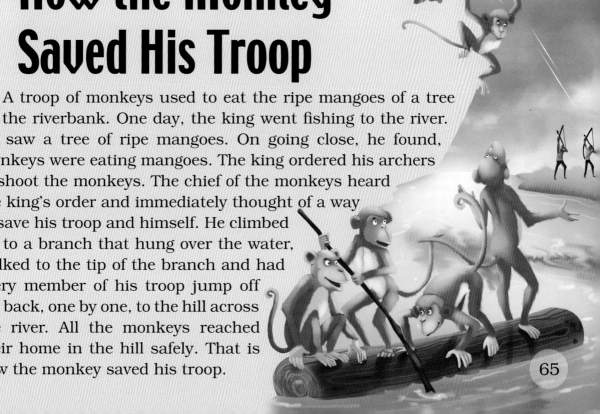

65

7 The Fighting Cocks and the Eagle

Some time ago, two cocks were fighting over a dunghill. Each of them two was fighting with all their strength to defeat the other, because the winner would be the ruler of the dunghill. At long last, one cock won as the other one fell after getting wounded severely. The beaten one crept into a hen's house. The winner flew up to a loft and crowed at the top of his voice to announce his success. Then an eagle was flying by. He darted down on the cock and carried him away. Witnessing the whole thing from the hen's house, the other cock came out and took his position. He announced himself to be the ruler. Pride goes before defeat.

8 The Goatherd and the Wild Goats

Once upon a time there was a goatherd who lived with his flock. One day, he was guiding his flock through a strong snowstorm. He could hardly see anything through the darkness. So he went into a cave where some wild goats were already standing inside. They also took refuge there. The goatherd saw the big, stout wild goats and liked them. He felt disgusted of the skinny domestic goats that he was guarding. So he, instead of feeding his own goats, gave the leaves to the wild ones. The next morning, he found his own goats perishing of hunger and the wild goats running out of the cave. Whoever neglects old friends for the sake of new deserves what he gets if he loses both.

9 The Goat and the Panther

A goatherd was taking his goats up the mountain to graze. While the goats were climbing up the mountain, a young goat got left behind. Nervously trying to catch up with others, she noticed a panther hiding behind the bushes. The goat thought of a plan to save herself. She went to the panther and said, "Good day to you, Uncle. You've always been very nice to us. My mother too sends her greetings to you." The panther looked at her in surprise and said, "Do you think I'll let you go if you call me uncle?" The goat then pleaded for her life. But the panther took no pity on the goat and pounced on her. The poor goat could not outwit the panther.

10 The Story of the Crows

There lived a crow and his wife on a tree near the sea. "This is so nice," cheered the she-crow while bathing in the sea. The moment she uttered those words, a huge wave came and swept her away. "Oh! My wife has been washed away by the cruel waves," cried the he-crow. Hearing him, the other crows came running in. An elderly crow suggested, "Let's empty the sea water and save her. We need not fear the sea as we are superior beings." So the crows started drawing out the sea water with their beaks, singing proudly: 'We're the mighty lot. We will save our friend, and set a heroic trend.'

Hearing their words, the sea spirit became angry and swept them all away with a huge sea wave. It's not wise to challenge one stronger than you.

11 The Horse

Once upon a time, there lived a horse who owned a whole meadow. One day, when the horse was away, a stag came galloping in and damaged the entire pasture. When the horse came back, he found everything destroyed and was very angry.

He wanted to teach the stag a lesson, so he went to a man. "Can you please help me punish the wild stag?" asked the horse. The man said, "Yes. But tell me one thing. Will you let me climb your back and ride on you? Then I can punish the stag with a weapon in hand."

The horse said, "Why not? I'm ready."

Since then the horse, instead of gaining revenge on the stag, is working as a slave of man.

12 How the Turtle Saved His Life

A king once built a pool for his young sons to play in. He ordered his men to put some fish into it. Quite by chance, the men also put in a turtle. The princes ran away in fright when they first saw it. The king ordered his men to kill the turtle. But they did not know how to. After much discussion, a guard said, "Throw it into the water where it flows out over the rocks into the river. Then, it will surely be killed." The turtle popped his head out of his shell and said, "You can throw me directly into the river in order to kill me!" The guards threw it into the water instead. The turtle laughed as he swam back home.

13 The Ass and Its Driver

An ass was being driven by his master. Suddenly, he broke free from the cart and ran frantically out of the trodden track. As he was running without direction, he ended up reaching a steep cliff. There was a deep valley below the cliff. Just when he was about to move a step forward, his master grabbed his tail and pulled him back. The ass also struggled to break free from the master. The master tried to drag him back with all his might. The master wanted to save the ass but the ass was blind to his fate. At last, the master let him go. "I quit. If you want to be your own master, I must let you go. A willful beast must go his own way." And so the ass jumped foolishly to his own end.

14 The Wolf and the Horse

A wolf was roaming near a meadow. He entered a field of oats. However, even after much effort, he could not eat a single oat.

As he went out of the field, he came across a horse. He told him, "Friend, I have found many oats there in the field. They are splendid in quality. I have saved all for you. Please come. They are all yours."

The horse smiled and said, "O my dear fellow, if you could eat oats, I think you would have been concerned only with your stomach and give no thought to me. Do you expect me to thank you? You gave away oats only because they were of no use to you. So I don't need to express gratitude to you."

15 The Cure and the Crows

Once, a king called for his royal doctor to cure his ill elephants. On the way to the palace, the doctor lay down in the shadow of tree. Suddenly, a crow's droppings fell on his forehead! He grew very angry and vowed to kill all the crows.

When he reached the king, he suggested, "Rubbing the crows' fat on the wounds only will heal the elephants." The king ordered that all the crows be killed to make the medicine. There began a great killing of crows. The leader of the crows rushed to the king and pleaded, "Please don't kill us. The fact is that crows don't have any fat." The king realized his mistake and ordered harsh punishment for the wicked royal doctor.

16 The Lark

Seeing a bird-catcher setting a trap, a lark who was sitting at a branch of a tree asked, "Man, what you are up to? What are you doing here?"

The bird-catcher said, "I'm setting up a colony. I am laying the foundations for my city."

After he had done his work, the bird-catcher went to a distance, and hid himself behind a bush.

The lark had believed the bird-catcher and did not know the reality. He flew down to the net and took up the bait. Immediately, he found himself caught in a noose. The bird-catcher came from behind the bush and grabbed him.

The lark said, "How nice a man you are! If this is the nature of your city, you'll hardly find any settlers here."

17 The Great Horse Knowing-One

The Bodhisattva once served the king of Benaras as a strong and wise horse. The king named him Great Knowing-One, for he could sense his rider's thoughts. Once, Benaras was attacked by seven neighbouring states. The bravest of the king's knights rode on Great Knowing-One. Great Knowing-One suggested to the knight, "Sir, let's not kill any of the enemy kings and capture them alive. I'll help you to do that." Saying so, Great Knowing-One stormed through the enemy cavalries. The knight captured the seven kings. But in that process, Great Knowing-One was wounded and died. Before dying, the noble horse pleaded with his king to pardon the seven enemy kings. The king did as the horse wished and pardoned the kings and set them free. The enemy kings turned friends.

18 The Mighty Fish

A long time ago, there lived a kind, pious fish. Then, there was terrible drought. The lake dried up and many water creatures lost their lives. Seeing the great danger they were all facing, the pious fish decided to do something to save himself and the others.

One day, ignoring all risks, the pious fish made his way through the mud and came up to the surface. There he called upon the Rain God and prayed, "O lord! Pardon our sins. Please send rain and relieve us from this misery."

Such was his cry that it shook everything from hell to heaven and God's heart filled with compassion. He sent heavy rains to the earth and thus the great fish and his companions were saved.

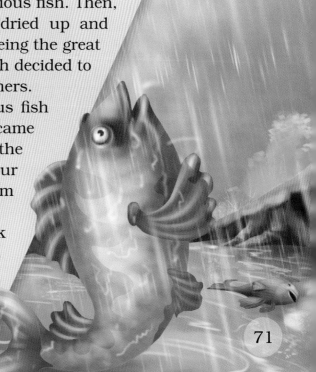

19 The Hunter Who Killed the Monkeys

Once, the Bodhisattva was born as a monkey named Nandiya. His mother was old and blind. Nandiya was a dutiful son. They lived under a banyan tree in a forest near the village. One day, a hunter came to the forest. He wanted to kill the old mother. Her son resisted the hunter. "Don't kill my helpless mother. Spare her life and take mine instead," he pleaded. "You fool! You're young. Why did you have to come in the way? Now both you and your mother will die," said the hunter and killed them both.

On his way back home, he heard that lightning had hit his house and all members of his family died. God had punished him for the sin he committed by killing the monkeys.

20 The Saintly Hare

The Bodhisattva was once born as a pious hare. One evening, he remembered that the coming day was the auspicious day on which guests were offered food.

The Bodhisattva had no food that was good enough for a guest. After much thought, he decided to offer his body as food to anyone who may come to visit him. Sakka, the king of gods, learning about Bodhisattva's resolve, appeared to test his strength of character. He took the guise of a brahmin and pretended to be in need of food. The Bodhisattva then lit a fire by striking two stones and jumped into the raging flames. Sakka was stunned by this act of sacrifice. Sakka, in his honour, adorned the moon with the hare's image.

21 The Elephant Lajjalu

Once, a gentle king had an elephant who was shy. His name was Pe Lajjalu, which means a shy being.

One night, he heard some robbers, who said, "A thief must beat anyone. He should never be merciful." On listening to their inhuman talk, Lajjalu thought, "These men have come to teach me. I must follow their advice."

Next day, he caught a keeper up with his trunk, and threw him up in the air. Lajjalu's nature had changed. One day, the worried king heard a priest saying, "Good company can reform wicked behaviour."

The king asked sages and priests to instruct Lajjalu. The holy men said to Lajjalu, "We should never hurt anyone."

Lajjalu thought, he must follow the instructions of the teachers, and his behaviour changed for good.

22 The Antelope and the Hunter

Once, a hunter discovered that while all the other animals ate fruits from all the trees of the forest, an antelope ate only from one particular tree. He soon came up with a plan to catch the antelope and placed some fruits below the tree as bait. He then kept the noose trap open and hid behind the branches of the tree.

When the antelope arrived, he wondered, "How come there are so many fruits lying here today!" Then he saw the hunter hiding behind the branches! Pretending not to have seen him, the antelope cried aloud, "Since my favourite tree is behaving in a strange way, I will get fruits from another tree!" Saying this, the wise antelope ran away, while the hunter cursed his luck.

23 The Hermit and the Elephant

Once, a hermit found a baby elephant in the forest. He cared for him like his own child. As time passed, the hermit became very fond of the elephant and named him Somadatta. They both loved each other. One day, the hermit brought a lot of bananas home, then left for the village. While he was away, Somadatta ate all the bananas out of greed. Soon, his stomach became so big that it burst and he died. When the hermit returned and found his beloved Somadatta dead, he wept bitterly hugging the elephant's corpse. The Bodhisattva, a wise man, saw the hermit and said, "Don't lament. One who is born is sure to die. It's only your attachment which is the cause of your sorrow." The hermit realized the truth of his life and overcame his sorrow.

24 The Banyan Deer

There lived two herds of deer in a forest. They were called the Banyan Deer and the Monkey Deer. The king of that country regularly hunted deer for meat. To save them from being hunted, the leaders of two herds decided to send one deer to the king every day. One day, it was the turn of a member of the herd of Banyan Deer who had a young baby. She went to the leader and requested him to save her life. So, the leader decided to go to the king instead of her. When the king saw him, he asked, "You are the leader! Why did you come?" The Banyan-Deer then explained why he had come. The king was moved with the kindness of the leader and promised he would never eat a deer again.

25 The Story of a Tigress

The Bodhisattva was once born as a scholar. He became an ascetic with many disciples. One day, while the Bodhisattva was walking through the forest with his disciple Ajita, he saw a hungry tigress about to eat her own cubs.

Deeply moved, the Bodhisattva decided to offer himself as food for the tigress. He thus sent Ajita away on some pretext and placed himself in front of the tigress. The tigress ripped him apart and fed on him with her cubs.

When Ajita returned and saw his master's blood stained clothes, he shouted out in terror, "Good Gracious! These are Master's clothes. That means these creatures must have fed on him…" With a heavy heart, Ajita returned to narrate how his master had sacrificed his life out of charity and compassion.

26 The Jewelled Serpent

Once, Nagraj, the king of the serpents, disguised himself as a human being and visited the hermitage of a sage. The hermit welcomed him warmly and soon they became very close friends.

Since then, Nagraj frequently visited the hermitage. But one day, Nagraj visited him in his original form and this scared the hermit. "If you want to avoid Nagraj then ask for his dearest possession and he is sure to go away for-ever," advised the sage's friend. Next day, the sage asked for the wish-fulfilling gem that Nagraj carried on his head. He kept pleading for it until one day Nagraj, getting irritated, said, "You ask too much from me, so I shall never come to you again."

Thus, the sage went back to his peaceful ascetic life, with nothing to fear from.

27 Lord Sakka and His Dog Mahakanha

In the reign of King Usinara, the people of the earth left the path of virtue and took to immoral ways. Sakka, the king of gods, decided to bring them back to the rightful path. He disguised himself as a forester, and Matali, the heavenly charioteer, turned himself into a fierce black dog called Mahakanha. Together, they reached the gates of Usinara's kingdom.

"Grrr...," roared the fierce dog as he approached the palace. Terrified, all the men fled into the city. Sakka said to the frightened king, "This dog is hungry and will devour all those who commit sins." Finally, Sakka revealed his identity and returned to his heavenly abode. From then on, the king and his people left the wrongful path and took to truth and virtue.

28 The Old Hound

A hound served his master well when he was young and strong. As time passed by, the hound grew old and lost strength. One day, while hunting for a beast with his master, he caught a boar. But as the hound had lost its teeth, it was difficult for him to hold on the boar. When the master arrived at the spot, he was furious to find his faithful beast unsuccessful in its mission. He started beating him savagely. The beast raised his face and in a feeble voice said, "Master! Spare me. You know it well that I have lost neither my courage nor my will. It's really sad that I am not physically strong any longer. But it's a fact that I have lost my strength and teeth in your service."

29 The Mouse Merchant

Once, a man picked up a dead mouse hearing the royal advisor's remark that he could make a fortune out of it. He sold it to a shopkeeper who wanted it for his cat in exchange for a copper coin. The man bought some cakes with the coin and sold them to some flower pickers for a good price. Then he prospered and opened a sweetshop.

He gifted the royal advisor a thousand gold coins to thank him for the good advice. Seeing how hardworking the man was, the royal advisor gave his daughter in marriage to the man. He was now the son-in-law of the royal advisor. After the royal advisor's death, the king appointed the man as the next royal advisor and he no longer remained an ordinary man.

30 The Story of the Sarabha

The Bodhisattva was once born as Sarabha, who was a forest deer with the strength of a lion and the wisdom of a man. The Sarabha was kind and compassionate.

One day, the king went hunting and aimed at Sarabha. The Sarabha ran speedily as he had vowed to avoid violence.

The king followed him on his horse. They went deep into the forest and came to a deep crack in the earth, which the Sarabha leapt across easily. But the king's horse could not leap over it and the king and his horse fell headlong into the deep crack. The Sarabha saw this and feeling sorry for the king, pulled him out of the deep crack.

The king realized that the compassionate Sarabha was not an ordinary deer and with great respect sought the Sarabha's forgiveness.

1 The Brahmin and the Goat

Once, long ago, there lived a brahmin. One day, he was carrying a goat on his shoulders and was going towards his home. As he was walking along, two thieves spotted him. The thieves were the part of a gang that worked in a planned manner. Their every move and action used to be planned and coordinated. When the thieves saw the goat with the brahmin, the first thing that came to their mind was how to cheat the poor brahmin by taking his goat away. They could not have robbed him as it was day time and they were on a very busy street. However, the thieves continued to pursue the brahmin, waiting to catch him at a lonely spot. The distance from the market place to his home was quite long. After walking some distance, the brahmin had to go through a stretch of forest to reach his home. The forest was lonely and there was no one on the path. The thieves thought that the forest would be the ideal place for them to cheat the brahmin. Their plan was ready now. The two thieves placed themselves separately in the forest, so that no one could think that they were working together.

Their plan to trick the brahmin into parting with his goat was ready. They were only waiting for the right opportunity to implement their plan. One of the thieves stepped into his path. The thief said with an expression of shock on his face, "Why are you carrying such a dirty dog on your shoulders?"

The brahmin got angry. "Are you blind?" He snapped at the thief. "Can't you see that I am carrying a goat?" "I don't see a goat, I see a dog," said the

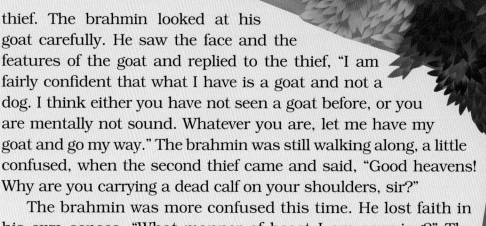

thief. The brahmin looked at his goat carefully. He saw the face and the features of the goat and replied to the thief, "I am fairly confident that what I have is a goat and not a dog. I think either you have not seen a goat before, or you are mentally not sound. Whatever you are, let me have my goat and go my way." The brahmin was still walking along, a little confused, when the second thief came and said, "Good heavens! Why are you carrying a dead calf on your shoulders, sir?"

The brahmin was more confused this time. He lost faith in his own senses. "What manner of beast I am carrying?" The Brahmin thought in panic. "Perhaps it is a demon that can change its form." He threw the goat off his shoulders, and scampered away home. The thieves quickly grabbed the goat they wanted.

One should use one's own intelligence when judging any situation.

2 The Girl Who Married a Snake

Once, a brahmin's wife gave birth to a baby, but the child came to be a snake. The brahmin's wife didn't care that her infant was a snake. She brought up the snake with love and care. When the snake grew up she began to think of getting her son married. But the question was, which girl would marry a snake?

One day, the brahmin told his friend that he was looking for a bride for his son. The friend promised his daughter's hand in marriage. Thus, the girl and the snake got married. Every night, the young man would come out of the snake's skin and would stay with his wife.

One night, the brahmin saw the snake turning into a young man. He rushed into the room, seized the snake's skin and threw it into the fire. The young man said, "Due to a curse, I had to remain a snake until somebody without asking me, destroyed the snake's body." Thus, the young man never became snake again and lived happily with his wife.

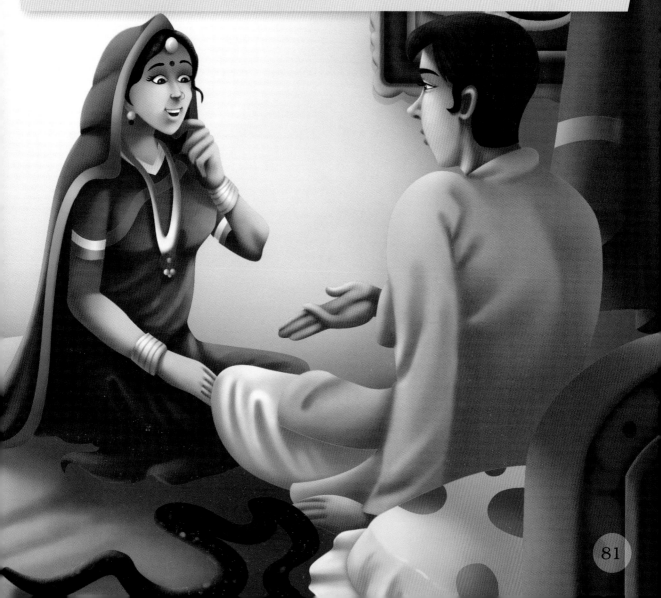

3 The Wise Minister

Once upon a time, a minister of a state invited the king to the wedding ceremony of his daughter. When the king arrived with the royal family, he guided him to the special seat arranged for the king. Once they reached there, the minister was embarrassed to find the sweeper sitting there. He pulled him up and scolded him publicly. The sweeper felt humiliated and planned to take revenge. Next morning, when he was sweeping the king's chamber, he deliberately muttered, "O the innocent king, I pity he does not know the juicy topic about the minister and the queen." The king, who was half asleep, sprang up. "What the hell are you saying?" asked he. "O sir, I had a sleepless night. I was in a daze," said the sweeper. But this was enough to put the seed of suspicion in the king's mind. After he left, the king said to himself, "The sweeper can be the most authentic source of such news. He visits all the rooms of the palace." The king started snubbing the minister. One day he even

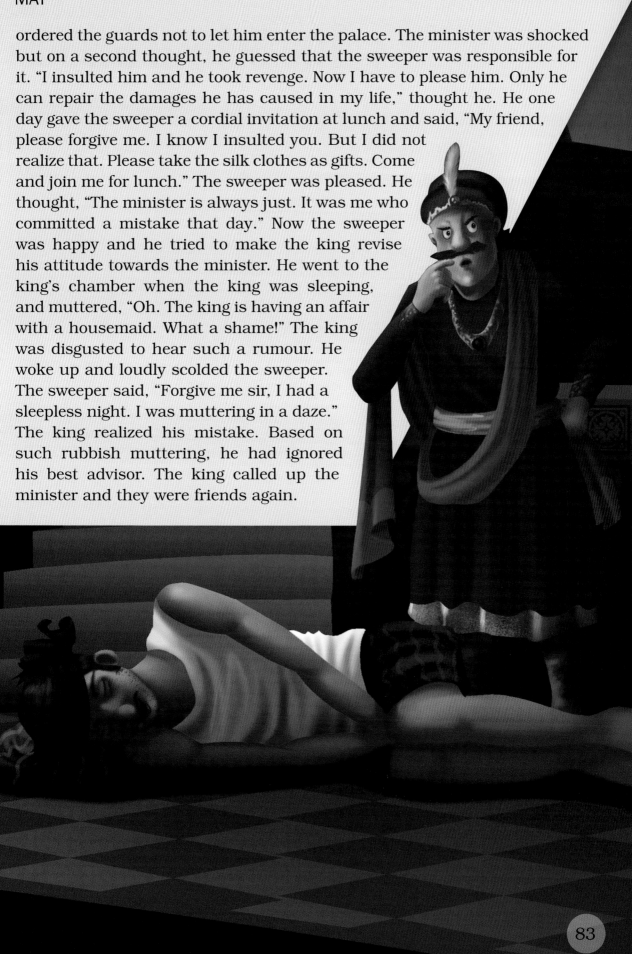

ordered the guards not to let him enter the palace. The minister was shocked but on a second thought, he guessed that the sweeper was responsible for it. "I insulted him and he took revenge. Now I have to please him. Only he can repair the damages he has caused in my life," thought he. He one day gave the sweeper a cordial invitation at lunch and said, "My friend, please forgive me. I know I insulted you. But I did not realize that. Please take the silk clothes as gifts. Come and join me for lunch." The sweeper was pleased. He thought, "The minister is always just. It was me who committed a mistake that day." Now the sweeper was happy and he tried to make the king revise his attitude towards the minister. He went to the king's chamber when the king was sleeping, and muttered, "Oh. The king is having an affair with a housemaid. What a shame!" The king was disgusted to hear such a rumour. He woke up and loudly scolded the sweeper. The sweeper said, "Forgive me sir, I had a sleepless night. I was muttering in a daze." The king realized his mistake. Based on such rubbish muttering, he had ignored his best advisor. The king called up the minister and they were friends again.

4 The Selfish Swans

There was a kind-hearted king in whose pond in the palace, lived swans of golden colour. They led a luxurious life. They used to give the king their golden feather each month. One day, there came a migratory bird. The swans became jealous of it. "See the bird is pure golden in colour. He is bound to get preference. We must chase the bird away if we need to remain important," they said to one another.

Suddenly, the king's men saw the swans attacking the bird. The king rushed out of palace and saw the violent scene.

"Catch those swans and cage them. They are now jealous of the guest bird," the king said angrily.

The swans flew away from the vicinity. Jealousy robbed them of all they had.

5 The Peacock and the Crane

There lived a peacock beside a lake. He had beautiful feathers that he admired. One day, a crane came to stay there. The peacock said, "I am glad to welcome you to this place." Now, the peacock spread its feathers. The colourful feathers looked beautiful in the bright sunlight. It reflected in the water of the lake. It was in the full glory of its beauty.

The proud peacock said, "Look at my feathers. They are so beautiful and special. Far more beautiful than yours." The crane understood the tone.

He said, "Whatever I have, I can fly with it. Your beauty is useless because your feathers don't help you to fly." The curt remark brought the peacock down to the ground of reality. It made him humble.

6 The Holy Man and the Rich Mouse

Once, there lived a holy man. One day, a friend visited him. The friend wanted to talk, but the holy man kept making noise with a bamboo stick. "We meet after a long time but you are not interested in conversation," said his friend. The holy man said, "No my friend! Actually I am warding off the mouse, who eats the meal I save. Come, let's find it." The two men searched the hole of the mouse. When they found it, they dug it up and found the load of meal the mouse had accumulated. They immediately took it away.

When the mouse returned home, there was no food for him. He lost all his energy and stopped moving out. So, the holy man got rid of the mouse.

7 The Wicked Crow

There once lived a heron, who was into the bad company of a wicked crow. One day, a traveller was resting in the cool shade of a tree.

As the sun moved to the west, the man's face was exposed to the blazing sunlight. The heron took pity at the man, so he spread his wings to guard the man's face. But his friend, the crow, was trying to hinder the man in sleep. When the man was yawning, he quickly relieved himself right into his mouth and flew away.

The man woke up and looked around. He found the heron and thought it was the one who did it. In anger, he shot the bird dead. One suffers for the evil company he keeps.

8 The Poor Cat

A cat fell in love with a man and prayed to Venus to turn her into an attractive girl. The goddess granted her prayer. Now she was a beautiful girl. The young man fell in love with her. Soon, he took her home as a bride. The goddess was curious to know whether the cat has adapted all kinds of possible humanly qualities. So, she put her to a test. She set a mouse in the house that started running to and fro. This was too much for the girl. She forgot about her new shape and like a cat, pounced on the mouse. Shocked at her action, the goddess once again changed her into a cat. Try as one may, it is impossible to change one's nature.

9 Two Fighting Rams

In a jungle there lived a wolf. One day, he came across two rams fighting violently.

The wolf stopped there and thought, "If the two rams get killed in the bloody fight, I will be the gainer. I can eat their flesh and taste their blood." Both the rams were severely injured while fighting. Blood gushed out from their injuries. It tempted the wolf. He went ahead to lick the blood from their injuries. The rams were so much engrossed in their fight that they could not even notice the wolf.

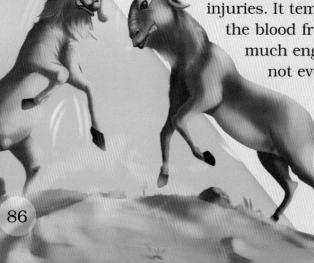

The impatient wolf greedily licked their blood. He, poked his head between the battling beasts.

And all of a sudden he was crushed to a shapeless pulp of flesh. He died for his impatience and folly.

10 The Arab and The Camel

A man was once about to set out for a long journey across the Arabian Desert. Before leaving, he spent quite some time preparing his luggage. Thereafter, he loaded all he wanted to take with him on the back of the camel. When the preparations for the journey were over, he asked the camel whether he would prefer going uphill or downhill. The camel listened to him carefully and calculated the weight put on him. After a while, the camel asked his master, "Sir, is there a third option of undertaking a journey straight across the plain? If it is possible then, I'll be happy to take that route only. Given the weight of the luggage I am carrying, I think the easiest route should be preferred."

11 The Ram's End

Once upon a time, a ram used to stay in a village. One day, he went to the forest and discovered a lot of greenery. He ate to the full, but could not find the way out of the forest. So, he had to stay there. Others in the forest were scared of his looks. He had twisted horns. The lion too was scared to see such a beast. He thought, "He must be stronger than me. I have to keep away from him." Later, the lion saw the ram eating leaves. The lion understood the nature of the beast. "Oh! My fear was meaningless. This beast is weaker than me," said the lion to himself.

The lion pounced on the ram and killed him in no time.

12 The Archer and the Lion

A skilled archer went into a forest for hunting. All the beasts in the forest were frightened at his sight. Only a lion stayed back and challenged him to fight.

The archer immediately launched an arrow and in a loud voice said, "See my messenger has something to tell you." The lion was wounded by the arrow. He ran away as fast as he could.

A fox, who had seen it all happen, came to the lion and said, "Don't run away. Why don't you stay and fight him." The lion said, "No my friend. If a messenger can hurt you so much, think what the man who had sent him can do! It's dangerous to have a neighbour who can easily strike from a distance."

13 The Woman and the Fat Hen

Once upon a time, there was an old woman, who had a hen. The hen used to lay an egg everyday, which she sold at a good price. One day, the woman thought, "Oh! The hen is giving me an egg a day. She must give two eggs a day, if I double her food. And I will be able to sell more eggs and will earn more. I will become rich one day!" She then started feeding the hen more and more. The hen grew so fat and contended that she stopped laying eggs altogether. Now the woman was not able to get even one egg a day. She repented over what she did. Calculations do not always produce good result.

14 The Sly Fox

Once, a fox saw a deer. The sly fox called a mouse for help, joined later by a tiger, they planned to kill the deer.

The mouse nibbled the deer's feet, while the tiger pounced upon him and killed the deer.

The fox said, "We do not eat anything before taking bath. I have taken the bath. Now it's your turn to take bath." When the tiger returned after his bath, the fox said, "The mouse is boasting that it was solely for him that we have food." The tiger's pride was hurt and he went away.

When the mouse came, he said, "I challenged the tiger for a fight, he fled. Now it's your turn." The mouse vanished from the spot. The fox ate the flesh all alone.

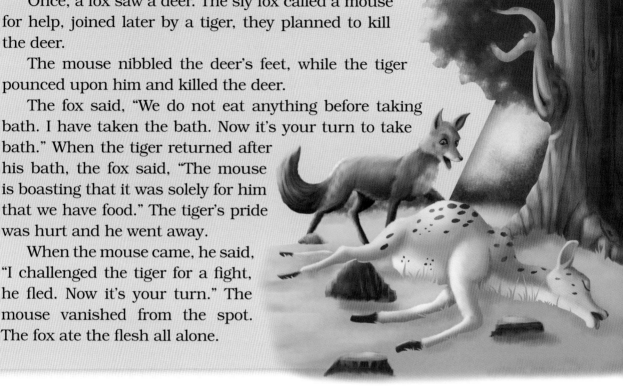

15 The Fox and the Grapes

A hungry fox was roaming in the jungle. Suddenly, he came across a place where ripe, juicy grapes hung high on the vines. He said to himself, "These must be tasty. I should eat them." The grapes hung higher than he could reach. So he jumped high to try to reach those fruits but in vain. He kept on jumping high to gain access to the juicy, ripe bunch but he failed each time. He tried again and again but failed everytime. When he got tired and realized that he had to give up, he retreated and said to himself, "O! I really don't need those grapes. Those were sour." The behaviour of the fox shows that one finds it easy to despise the thing that one cannot get.

16 The Crooked Eagle

Once, an eagle lived on the branch of a tree, while a fox lived in the hole of the same tree.

One day, when the fox left the hole, the eagle went down to the hole and took the fox-cubs to feed his offspring. When the fox returned home, he pleaded to the eagle to return the cubs. Thinking that his nest was too high for the fox to reach, the eagle ignored his request. The fox went to a temple nearby and brought a fire-lit torch. He immediately set the tree on fire. The heat and the smoke frightened the eagle. For the safety of his own kids, he flew down to the fox and returned him his cubs. It is true that a tyrant is never safe from the ones he oppresses.

17 The Boy and the Scorpion

Once upon a time, a young boy was catching locusts on a wall. He had caught many locusts but he was trying for more. When he noticed a scorpion in their midst, he mistook it for another locust. The boy went ahead to pick the scorpion from the wall, but suddenly the scorpion pointed his sting at the boy, ready to bite him, and said, "Don't ever try to catch me like the poor locusts. If you try you will wash your hand of your locusts and your life too." This fable shows that you should not treat bad people the same way that you treat good people; rather, you should deal with each of them in the way that suits their character.

18 The Kid and the Wolf

A kid once strayed from the herd and was lost in the jungle. A wolf saw him and began to pursue him. To escape certain death, the kid thought out a plan. He turned back at the wolf and said, "I know I am going to be your victim. Before that, I want to make it merry and want to dance. Will you please pipe a tune for me? I want to dance for the last time in my life." The wolf started piping tune and the boy danced on. The tune reached the dogs' ears and they rushed to spot to find out the source of the music. They found the wolf and killed him. The wolf was killed because, though he was cruel, he lacked intelligence.

19 The Foolish Pigeons

Once upon a time, there was a hungry hawk that chased a flock of pigeons, who always managed to fly to safety. The pigeons remained scared of the hawk, always alert to the possible attacks of the fierce bird. The desperate hawk, who wanted to prey on them for a long time, hit on a plan and went to the pigeons, saying, "What's the use to lead such a life in fear? Better make me the king of your clan so that I can protect you against the dangers." The pigeons felt inspired. They thought the hawk is interested in their welfare. They made the hawk their king.

Immediately after becoming their leader, the hawk started eating the pigeons one by one.

Some remedies are worse than dangers.

20 The Foolish Friend

Once, a king appointed a monkey as his bodyguard. One day, when the king was resting. The monkey stood over the king's bed, looking around watchfully. A little later, a fly flew into the room and buzzed around over the sleeping king. The monkey waved his hands and drove the fly away. But again the fly returned. The monkey shooed it away again. But the fly flew back again. This time, the monkey decided to teach it a lesson. He seized the king's sword, and when the buzzing fly sat upon the king's neck, he brought the sword down in order to cut the fly into two. The fly escaped and the poor unsuspecting king was cut into two. Sometimes, a foolish friend does more harm than a wise enemy.

21 Story of Sabbadatha, the Jackal

Once, the young Bodhisattva got to know a spell capable of subduing the world. One day, while he was reciting the spell, a jackal learned it. With its help, the jackal subdued all the creatures in the forest and became their king under the name Sabbadatha. Then, he invaded the city by making all lions roar. He sat astride a lion which in turn stood on the back of two elephants. The Bodhisattva asked everyone to stuff their ears with flour so that the lion's roars wouldn't reach them. The lions let out their earth-shaking roar. Being terrified, the elephants dropped them from their back. Sabbadatha fell to the ground and got trampled under the elephants' feet. He who uses knowledge for a wrong purpose brings about his own ruin.

22 The Ant and the Grasshopper

One summer day, a grasshopper was singing and hopping about, enjoying his freedom. He saw an ant that was busy storing grain for the winter.

The grasshopper said, "We can sing some songs and dance while the sun shines." "Oh no," said the ant. "Winter is coming. I am storing up food for the winter. I think you should do the same." The grasshopper said, "Winter is a long time off. There is plenty of food." So the grasshopper continued to dance while the ant continued to work. When winter came the grasshopper had no food and was starving. He went to the ant's house and asked, "Can I have some food?" "You danced last summer," said the ant in disgust. "You can continue to dance." And she gave him no food.

23 The Fawn and His Mother

Once a young fawn and his mother were taking a stroll through the forest. While walking, the young one asked his mother with a natural curiosity, "You are bigger than an average dog. You are strong as well. Not only that, you are even faster than many of the animal species. Besides, you have also got a strong pair of horns to defend yourself. Then, why do you run away when you hear a hound barking?" The mother smiled at the question of the kid and said, "I know what you say is true my son. But as soon as I hear a bark, I lose my head and take off as fast as possible. It's in my nature." No arguments will give courage to the coward.

24 The Wolf and the Lamb

A wolf saw a lamb and planned to eat him. They were standing by a small river. The wolf said to the lamb, "How dare you muddy the water I am drinking?" "The stream is flowing from your side," said the innocent lamb. "Okay!" said the wolf, adding, "But how will you explain your bad conduct last year? I heard you calling me names openly." Taken aback, the poor beast said, "I was not even born then." "Oh," the wolf made a small revision in his statement, and said, "then it should have been your mother. Be punished for the crime committed by your mother." Wasting no time, the wolf killed the lamb. A tyrant, always finds its excuse and those who are oppressed can never beat them in argument.

25 The Hunter and the Woodcutter

A hunter went into the jungle to hunt lions. When he entered the dense forest, he met a woodcutter there. The hunter asked the woodcutter, "My friend, have you seen any lion here?" The woodcutter replied, "Well, pal. I remember having seen its footprints somewhere not quite far from here. It means it will be near this place. Come along. Come with me. I'll show you the way." The hunter turned pale at the proposal. "No thanks friend," he said, "I'm happy to see its footprints. I don't want to track a lion. I am just tracking its footprints. Thanks for you help." Saying so, he took no time to leave the place.

It is easy for the coward to be hero at a distance.

26 The Lion and the Three Bulls

Once upon a time, there were three bulls. They were very good friends. They grazed together in one another's company and shared everything among themselves without malice or grudge. A lion had long been eyeing them for prey, but he knew as long as they were together, he could not match their collective strength.

So he hit a cunning plan to separate them from each other. He started spreading rumours about the bulls. The false rumours bred misunderstanding among them. Slowly and slowly they grew jealous of one another. And finally this resulted in disharmony and they started living separately forever. It was a golden opportunity for the lion and he did not waste it. He killed them one by one and ate them. Unity is strength.

27 The Leopard and the Fox

A leopard and a fox were living together in a jungle. They were good friends and had never had any quarrel on trifles and petty issues. However, one day, it so happened that they had a heated discussion which eventually culminated in a contest to decide who was more handsome of the two. The leopard first insisted that he was more handsome as he had an unusual bright yellow coloured body. He therefore boasted of his innumerable black spots. The fox listened to him attentively and agreed. Then, after a brief pause, he said, "Yes, you are more beautiful than me. You have a spotted body and it's bright in colour. But I think my smart mind is more important than your beautiful body."

28 The Man Bitten by a Dog

A man was bitten by a dog. Blood gushed out of the deep wound. While he was suffering with pain he went to a number of people who he thought could give him the best piece of advice for the best treatment. Then, one of his friends came forward and said, "O friend, I have a way, which you may find useful. Go to the market. Buy a piece of bread. Dip it into the blood of your wound and throw it to the dog." The man who was bitten by the dog smiled at this. "No my friend, no. If I follow your suggestion, I will invite all the dogs of the city to bite me." Someone who proclaims to have overpowered his enemies never wants a supply of them.

29 The Old Lion

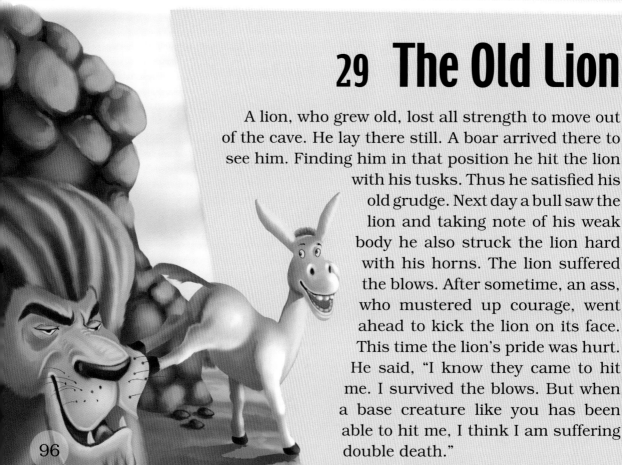

A lion, who grew old, lost all strength to move out of the cave. He lay there still. A boar arrived there to see him. Finding him in that position he hit the lion with his tusks. Thus he satisfied his old grudge. Next day a bull saw the lion and taking note of his weak body he also struck the lion hard with his horns. The lion suffered the blows. After sometime, an ass, who mustered up courage, went ahead to kick the lion on its face. This time the lion's pride was hurt. He said, "I know they came to hit me. I survived the blows. But when a base creature like you has been able to hit me, I think I am suffering double death."

30 The Swallow in the Chancery

A swallow once built her nest under the eaves of a court of justice. She and her little ones were happily living there. It was protected from all sides and they had no fear. But one day, something strange happened. A snake that was living nearby in his pit, slid out of his hole and ate all the offspring one by one. When the swallow returned home, she found her kids were gone! They were dead. Heavy at heart, the bird began to cry. On hearing her cries, a neighbour came there and tried to console her. The swallow said, "It's not only my little ones I mourn for, I am sorry for the fact that I am wronged at the very place to which the injured fly for justice."

31 Wolf in Disguise

There was a greedy wolf in a forest. He was always engaged in working out easy ways to earn a living. One day, he made a plan to mix into the flock of sheep. So, he took hide of a sheep and merged with the flock of sheep. Thereafter, he started grazing with the herbivorous animals. At night when the fold was closed the wolf too was locked in with them. The shepherd could not recognize the wolf as the wolf. So he was quite relaxed. But at night he ran short of food and came to take one of the sheep for dinner. Unfortunately, he took the wolf and carried him to the kitchen and killed it. Sometimes, the easy way serves more harm than profit.

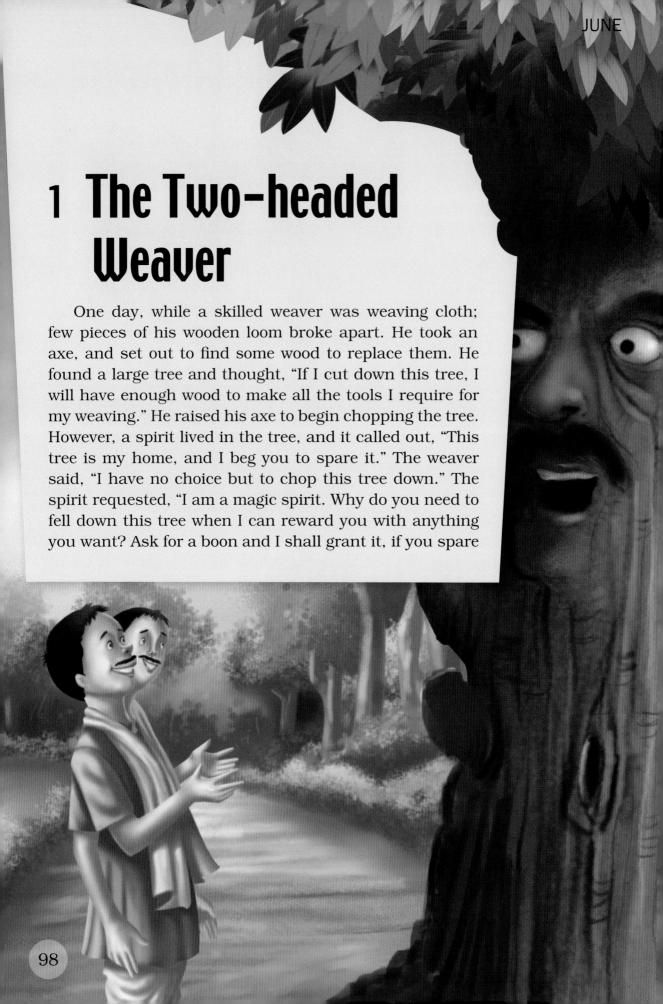

1 The Two-headed Weaver

One day, while a skilled weaver was weaving cloth; few pieces of his wooden loom broke apart. He took an axe, and set out to find some wood to replace them. He found a large tree and thought, "If I cut down this tree, I will have enough wood to make all the tools I require for my weaving." He raised his axe to begin chopping the tree. However, a spirit lived in the tree, and it called out, "This tree is my home, and I beg you to spare it." The weaver said, "I have no choice but to chop this tree down." The spirit requested, "I am a magic spirit. Why do you need to fell down this tree when I can reward you with anything you want? Ask for a boon and I shall grant it, if you spare

this tree!" The weaver was extremely happy to learn that he could have his wishes fulfilled and the wildest of his desires granted by this magic spirit. But, showing extreme caution, the weaver said, "I'll have to talk to my wife about this. Wait, till I return." Then he hurried to consult his wife.

On the way, he met his friend and asked for his opinion. The friend said, "Don't waste away this opportunity. You should demand a kingdom. You could rule it as a king and enjoy a rich and princely life." The weaver apparently liked the idea suggested by his friend, yet showing extreme care and precaution before demanding his wish from the magic spirit, he said, "Let me take my wife's opinion too." He hurried to his wife and told her everything. The weaver's wife replied sharply, "Your friend has given you a foolish advice. Don't pay attention to your friend's advice." She continued, "As a boon, you should ask for another

pair of arms, and a second head, so that you can work on two pieces of cloth at the same time. Soon you'll be famous and rich, from the skill of your own hands!"

The foolish weaver said joyfully, "I will do exactly as you say. You are my wife and I am sure you have given me the best advice I could have had." The weaver went back to the spirit and demanded, "Give me another pair of arms and another head immediately." He had barely uttered the words before he had another head and an extra pair of arms too.

The weaver ran towards his house excitedly, but as he approached it, the local people screamed in terror taking him as a dreadful demon. They beat him till he fell down dead. The poor weaver perished because he mindlessly followed the meaningless advice.

2 The Handsome Camel

One day, a poor villager discovered three camels—two kids and their mother. He took them to his home and started to look after them. He used to take them to forest for grazing and to river for bathing. He thought, "Let these camels grow, they will mate and I'll possess many more camels. Then I'll become a camel trader. Our poverty will come to an end." Whenever he used to ride the camels, his neighbours envied him. In some years, he had several camels. He became rich. Other villagers were jealous of him. One day, one of his jealous neighbours asked him, "How will you know which one is roaming where unless you tie a bell on the neck of one?" The carpenter tied a bell to the neck of one of the camels. One day, the camel with the bell was roaming in jungle. His bell tinkled continuously. A tiger heard the bell and pounced at him and made him his food. Thus, the carpenter suffered the loss as he blindly trusted a jealous neighbour.

3 The Seagull and the Hawk

Once, a seagull lived on the shore of a sea. He ate crabs and small fish, but never a big fish. One day, he wanted to catch fish for lunch. So, he pounced on a very large fish and gobbled it up. But it bloated his stomach so much that it started paining. At last he died of stinging pain in the stomach. As he lay dead on land, a hawk saw his corpse. He said to himself, "You deserve this fate. A bird of the air has no business to seek its food from the sea. But you didn't listen to me. Now you have learnt a lesson at the cost of your life. You did. And this is the result." Every man should be content to mind his own business.

4 Familiarity Brings Courage

One day, a fox saw a lion for the first time in his life. His long mane, formidable looks, scary roars and above all his stature as the king of the jungle frightened the weak beast. He almost fainted then and there. The next day when he again met the lion, he was still afraid but gathered courage to conceal his fear. He left the place as soon as possible. On the third day, the situation had completely changed. The fox went up straight to the lion and said, "Hello sir, hope everything is well." He started conversing with him on a personal note. He was no longer afraid of the lion and his past experience had made him familiar with the lion. Familiarity, thus, brings courage.

5 The Bear and the Fox

Once, all the animals in the jungle were discussing about human race. A bear was bragging of his excessive love and respect for the human race. He said, "I love human beings. I have befriended many of them and they all love me too. Now our friendship has gone to the level that they don't have fear of me, anymore." The other animals were listening to him with great interest. Then he went ahead and claimed that he never touched or mauled the human corpse. The fox was the listener of this boastful speech. He smiled at this and said, "It would have been more impressive had you said that you never ate a human being alive." We should never wait for a person to die to show respect to him.

6 The Cock Who Found a Jewel

Once, a cock felt hungry and went in search of food. He started scratching the ground in hope of finding grains for his meal. Meanwhile, he discovered a jewel deep in the mud. It was precious and big. The cock was surprised to see it. He lifted it and said to himself, "What a pretty jewel it is! It must be very precious. The world will run after it." After sometime he thought, "I am hungry and I need food. What will I do with a jewel? At this time, a grain is more precious to me because I can eat it. So the jewel is meaningless to me." He left the jewel there and started digging at another place. Actually, a thing is precious only if it is useful to you.

7 The Lamb and the Wolf

Once upon a time, there was a little lamb. The lamb was intelligent and careful. He faced threats from the other animals. One day, persuaded by a wolf, he took shelter in a temple. The wolf attempted to find him out in the temple but the lamb hid himself in such a safe place that the wolf could not reach him. So the wicked beast decided to influence the naïve little lamb with his words. In order to scare him out of the temple, he said, "Don't stay there, you poor little lamb. The priest will come and slay you." The lamb replied, "If it is so, so be it. I'll rather be sacrificed as a heifer to God than being a prey to a wicked beast like you."

8 The Ass and the Grasshoppers

Once upon a time, an ass became fascinated with the droning tune of the grasshoppers. The ass, therefore, wanted to develop a friendship with the grasshoppers. One day, he heard the chirping of some grasshoppers. Charmed by the low droning tune of the grasshoppers, he called them and asked showering praise on them, "My dear friend, you have a lovely voice. I am highly enchanted and desire to possess the same charms of melody as you possess." He asked further, "What do you eat so that you can sing so charming a tune?" The grasshoppers said, "We eat dew drops." In hopes of getting such a melodious voice, the ass started drinking dew drops and soon he died of hunger. It is said one man's medicine is poison to another.

9 The Creaking Wheels

Once, there was a pair of oxen who toiled day and night. They were tied to a wagon that they pulled. One day, the oxen were pulling the wagon along a bumpy road. They had to use all their strength to pull the wagon, but they did not complain. The wheels of the wagon were of a different sort. Though the task they had to do was very light compared with that of the oxen, they creaked and groaned at every turn. The driver of the wagon became furious. He said to the wagon, "Why do you make so much of noise while working? Can't you see the animals are doing their job in silence?" Those who cry the loudest are not the ones who are hurt the most.

10 A Lion in Love

A lion fell in love with a woodcutter's daughter. He went to the father of the daughter so that he could voice his intention to marry the little girl. The woodcutter was shocked at this proposal. In a bid to get out of the trouble, he hit upon a clever plan.

He said, "We are happy that a great creature like you wants to marry my daughter. But she is afraid of your claws and teeth. So, please get rid of those first. Then my daughter is all yours." Smitten with the girl, the lion got rid of his teeth and claws. After that, he went to the man's house to ask for his daughter's hands. The woodcutter was no longer afraid of the beast and he kicked him away.

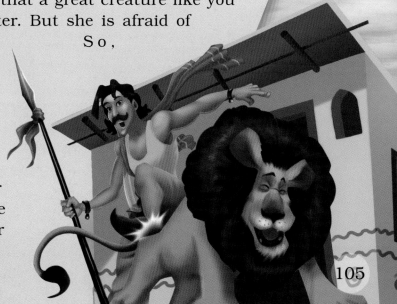

11 The Blind Man and the Whelp

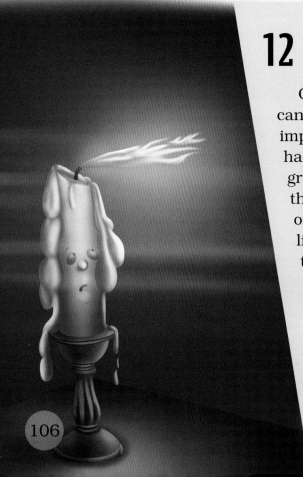

Once upon a time, a blind man had the rare capability of distinguishing any animal by simply touching it. One day, his friends decided to test his power. So, first they brought a cat to him and asked him to recognize what it was. The blind man touched the cat and said, "It is a cat." Then the friends brought a whelp of a wolf and gave it to him to tell them what it actually was. The blind man fumbled and fumbled but could not recognize the nature of the beast. He said, "I don't know whether you are a wolf or a dog, but I can say that whatever you are, I'll not trust you among a flock of sheep." Evil tendencies, in fact, are shown early in life.

12 The Candlelight

Once upon a time, there was a proud candlelight. The candle was full of his own importance and burned in its own glory. It had grown fat and saucy with too much grease and boasted of his light. It thought that it was brighter than the eternal source of light. He claimed to have the brighter light than the Sun and the Moon. While the arrogant light was boasting, a sudden puff of wind extinguished its illumination. Someone came and lit it again and said, "Keep shut you fool. The Sun and the Moon are perpetual sources of light and they are never extinguished like you. Yours one is but a spark of fire. One can light you or put you off at his own will."

13 The Crab and His Mother

One early morning, the mother crab took her son for a stroll along the beach. While he was walking, the mother asked, "Oh, my son, why do you walk sideways like that with your toes turned in?" The young crab said, "Can you please show me?" Mother crab was very glad to hear that her son was willing to learn. "I will show you, my son. Now step back and watch carefully," said the mother crab. With that, the mother crab stretched out one of her legs, turned her toes out and tried to take a step forward. But as soon as she did that, she tripped and fell flat on her nose! Do not tell others how to act unless you can set a good example.

14 The Dove and the Crow

Once upon a time, a dove in a cage was muttering to herself about the eggs she had hatched. A bird in cage has nothing really to be proud of than her motherhood. She was in fact boasting of her productivity and her motherhood. A crow was flying above the cage. He came down and perched on a branch of a nearby tree. Listening to the self-congratulatory tone of the dove, the crow was quite amused. He attracted the attention of the dove and said to her, "Cool down my dear friend. The more kids you have, the more slaves there will be for you to groan over. Nobody will be as happy as a normal free bird is." We must have freedom to enjoy our blessings.

107

15 The Little Mole

Once upon a time, a little mole lived with his mother. His mother took every possible care as the little mole was growing, but she did not readily believe whatever the little mole said. The little mole said to his mother, "Mother I can see." The mother heard this and was incredulous of him. So, to test whether her child was telling her the truth, the mother put a lump of frankincense before her and asked what it was.

The kid readily said, "Mother it's a stone." The mother coming to know the truth said, "Oh child, not only can't you see, but you can't smell even. You wanted to boast of one fake quality but eventually you exposed your defect." Brag about one defect, and you'll reveal another.

16 The Lion and the Bull

Once, a lion decided to trick a bull so he could eat him. He approached the Bull and said, "I have cooked a juicy sheep, my friend; come to my den, let's share a friendly meal." He thought when the bull would sit to eat, he would pounce upon him and kill him.

The bull agreed and they went to the lion's den. There, the bull saw a huge fire lighted and a large vessel of boiling water. He knew the lion was actually preparing to cook him!

Without saying a word the bull walked away. The lion rushed after him, asking why he was leaving.

"My dear friend," said the bull, "I am lazy but not silly. I can see no sign of a cooked sheep but I can see all the preparations for cooking a bull! Your trick will not work on me." And with that he left the lion standing hungry.

17 Like will Draw Like

Once upon a time there was a charcoal-burner. He had inherited a large house. This house had more rooms than he needed for himself. He felt lonely and isolated living alone in his huge house. So one day, he asked his friend to come and stay in his house permanently. His friend was a cloth-fuller whose job was to make the clothes white. But his friend happily rejected the offer. He said, "Thanks my friend, but I am sorry, I can't accept your offer. I can't live with you, as I am afraid as soon as I whiten my clothes, you will blacken them again, because it's your job. We may live together but unfortunately our professions will harm each other." Like will draw like.

18 The Swallow

Once upon a time, a swallow and a crow developed a friendship, but they used to argue over different issues. One day, they were in dispute as to which one of them was the finer bird. The crow claimed to be the finer one among the two birds, while the swallow did not agree at any cost. But they never reconciled at any point. The crow at last ended the dispute. He said, "Swallow, I know your feathers look beautiful and fine during summer, but it's a fact that my rough feathers, which are not so good-looking have lasted many winters. My feathers never looked beautiful to the eye but they have served me well during bad times." Fine-weather friends are not worth much.

19 The Quack Frog

Long ago, there was a frog. He remained, most of the time, under the muddy swamp. He had misconceived notions about his abilities to cure everyone. One day, he emerged out of the muddy swamp and claimed to cure all the diseases of the earth. "O friends, do visit me. I am bestowed with the miraculous power so that I can heal everyone's disease," he cried at the top of his voice. A fox was passing by. He stopped there and loudly said, "You are a quack doctor. If you are blessed with a miraculous power, why could you not cure your limping or your porous skin? So the self-proclaimed physician, heal yourself first. Man's professions can only be tested in his practice."

20 The Wolf and the Shepherds

In a village far away, there were some shepherds with their flock of sheep and goat. They were known to look after and protect their herd. However, they did not mind killing their animals for their meat. Once, a wolf took a quick glimpse into a hut only to discover them having a feast of mutton. The wolf smiled, and muttered to himself, "Oh, if the shepherd had discovered me in the same position, they would have bashed me to death. Now, see all of them are having a great feast of the flesh of the animals they are meant to protect from others. They are now doing the things they condemn others for doing." This is true that men often tend to condemn others for the very thing they do repeatedly.

21 The Thief and the Dog

There once lived a very faithful dog. The dog used to remain vigilant during the night, against intruders. One day, a thief came into the house. There, he came across this dog, who was as vigilant that night as always. The thief tried to bribe the dog with pieces of meat. The dog sniffed at it and barked out saying, "Get out you rogue. I had suspicions about you. But the excess kindness and generosity confirm my opinion that you are dishonest. You want to steal valuable things from my master's house. You can't bribe me and keep me shut. Only a devil tries to egg others in doing wrong deeds." A bribe in hand confirms mischief in mind.

22 The Eagle and the Arrow

Once upon a time, there was a happy and contended eagle. He had the habit of deeply analyzing situations and events taking place around him. Thus, he gained valuable knowledge. One day, he was perched on a high branch of a tree. Far down, on the ground lurked a bowman behind a bush. He took an aim at the eagle and shot him in the heart. The eagle, fatally wounded and dying with pain, found the arrow winged with the feathers of eagles. He came to realize the simple truth about life. He said, "How painful and fatal are the wounds made by the weapons we ourselves have supplied. Strangely these are taking our lives but these are made of our own feathers."

23 The Monkey and the Fishermen

A monkey was sitting on a high branch of a tree. He saw some fishermen setting nets in the river. As soon as they had done the first part of their job, they took a break and went to have some food. The monkey, eager to attempt something he had never done in his life, came down the tree and tried to set the net himself. In the process he unknowingly got entangled in the net. It nearly chocked him when he cried, "O poor me! It serves me right. I should never have meddled with something that had never been my business. I did it though I don't know the first things about fishing. And I am suffering for this." Don't do something you don't know about.

24 The Man and the Lion

Once upon a time, a man and a lion were travelling across the country. They were arguing about which one of them was braver and stronger. No one was willing to let the opponent have an upper hand. In their route, they came across a statue carved in stone depicting a lion being strangled by a man. The man, excited, cried out to the lion saying, "Now look at this. All have been proved. The statue tells the truth. We the men are stronger than you. History is telling the truth." The lion said, "That's your version of the story. If we were to build a statue on the same theme, it would depict twenty men struggling under a single paw of the lion." History is always written by the victors.

25 The Thirsty Pigeon

Once upon a time, there was a happy pigeon. During the summer, all lakes and ponds had dried up due to extreme heat. The pigeon was thirsty and desperate for water. But there was no water to be found anywhere. He came across a wall on which a sign of glass was painted upon a placard. The pigeon thought it was real and he swept down on it with all his might. He crashed against the board and wounded himself by breaking his wings. With stinging pain on the body, he fell flat on the ground and lay there helpless. After sometime a man who was passing by captured him. This is true when someone says that zeal should not outrun discretion, even when we are desperate.

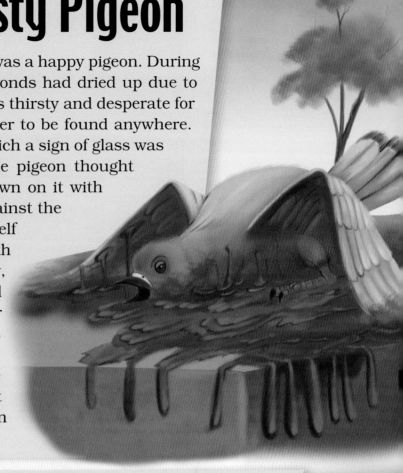

26 The Boy and the Nettle

Once upon a time, there was a young boy. He was a happy and fun loving child. He was an obedient child whose mother loved him. One day, the boy was playing in the field. He was suddenly stung by a nettle. He ran home. On meeting his mother he said that he had just touched a nasty little weed and was stung by it. His mother said, "It was just your touching that caused it to sting you my boy. But I must say this is not what it should be. I suggest that you grab the nettle firm in your hand the next time you see it. If you grab it hard it will not harm you ever." Whatever you do, do boldly.

113

27 The Wolf as a Friend

Once, a wolf was following a flock of sheep. Finding the shepherd close to the flock, he made no attempt to attack the gentle beast. The herdsman had his own suspicion and he guarded his sheep. Then, again the wolf showed his amiability and stayed with the sheep. Gradually, he became a part of the family. And the shepherd started trusting him. One day, the shepherd had to make his way to the town. He entrusted the wolf and left him to guard the flock. Once he left his place the wolf pounced at the sheep and devoured them one by one. On returning the shepherd understood what a fool he had been. He lamented for trusting a wolf. A friend like the wolf is worse than an enemy.

28 The Seaside Travellers

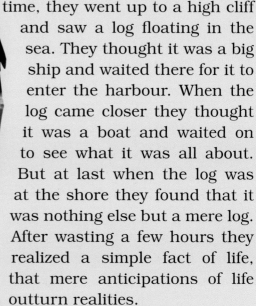

Once upon a time, there were some travellers waiting for a ship to arrive at a harbour. After waiting for a long time, they went up to a high cliff and saw a log floating in the sea. They thought it was a big ship and waited there for it to enter the harbour. When the log came closer they thought it was a boat and waited on to see what it was all about. But at last when the log was at the shore they found that it was nothing else but a mere log. After wasting a few hours they realized a simple fact of life, that mere anticipations of life outturn realities.

29 The Farmer and His Sons

A farmer had four sons. The brothers used to fight with each other. They did not stand by each other ever. The farmer was worried at this. The brothers lacked unity. So he decided to teach them a lesson. One day he called all of them and asked each one to try to break the bundle of sticks lying on the floor. Each of them tried to do so but they could not break it. Then the farmer untied the bundle and separated the sticks from each other. Then he asked his children to break a single stick each. All of them succeeded in this. The farmer said to his sons, "My sons. I want you to learn something from this. When the sticks were together, nobody of you could break them. Once they were separated, you broke each of them. You are like the sticks. Stay united and nobody can harm you. Unity is strength."

30 Shani, Mangal and Shukra

The planet gods Shani, Mangal and Shukra decided to find which one of them could make a perfect thing. Shani made a man. Mangal made a bull and Shukra made a house. They called Lord Narada to judge which of them is perfect. Narada started with the bull and found fault with its horns above his eyes. "This," he said, "does not enable the bull to see his own horns." The man, according to him, was faulty because he did not have windows in his chest so that his inward thought may come out. The house, lastly, was criticized as it lacked wheels and was not mobile. Listening to this, Shani said, "A fault-finder like you is never pleased. Stop criticizing others until you have made something worthwhile yourself."

115

1 The Sage's Daughter

Once upon a time, there was a sage who lived with his wife on the banks of a river. The couple had no children of their own and longed to have one. One day, when the sage was engaged in penance, a kite dropped a she-mouse in the lap of the sage. The sage decided to bring her home, but he changed her into a girl before he did so.

On seeing the girl, the sage's wife asked, "Who is she? Where did you bring her from?" The sage told her all that had happened. His wife was very happy, and she exclaimed, "You have given her life and so, you are her father. That way, I am her mother. God must have sent her to us because we are childless."

Soon the girl grew into a beautiful maiden. When she was sixteen, the couple decided to get her married. The sage prayed to the Sun God to come to him. When the latter appeared, the Sage asked him to marry his daughter.

However, the girl was not happy with the idea and said, "I am sorry, but I can't marry the Sun God, as he is burning hot." The disappointed sage then asked the Sun God himself to suggest a suitable groom for his daughter. The Sun God said, "The Lord of the Clouds could make a good match for her, as he is the only one who can protect her from the heat of the sun."

The sage then requested the Lord of the Clouds to marry his daughter. But the girl once again rejected the proposal, saying, "I don't want to marry a dark person like him. Besides, I am terrified of the thunder he sends out." The sage was disheartened again and asked the Lord of the Clouds to suggest a possible groom. The Lord of the Clouds said, "The Wind God can make a possible match for her as he can easily blow me away."

The sage then requested the Wind God to marry his daughter. This time too the girl declined the idea, saying, "I can't marry a frail person who is always blowing around." Deeply hurt and confused, the sage asked the Wind God to give his own suggestion. The Wind God replied, "The Lord of the Mountains is strong and stable and can stop the blowing wind easily. He would be a good choice."

117

The sage went to the Lord of the Mountains and asked him to marry his daughter. But the girl refused to accept him and said, "I can't marry someone who is too hard and cold." She asked the sage to find a softer husband for her. The sage sought the advice of the Lord of the Mountains. He replied, "A mouse will make a perfect match for her as he is soft and can easily make holes in any mountain."

This time the girl approved the idea. The sage was amazed and exclaimed, "How strange are the ways of destiny! You came to me as a mouse and I changed you into a human being. But being born a mouse you were destined to marry a mouse and fate has led you to this choice." He started praying and turned her back into a she-mouse.

Destiny can never be changed.

2 The Wise Fox

A hungry fox was roaming the forest when he saw a dead elephant. He jumped on it to have his fill, but his teeth could not penetrate the thick skin of the animal. He thought he would persuade a sharp-toothed beast to eat the elephant and then have the remaining flesh after he had had his share.

So he went to a lion and said, "Sir, I have killed an elephant. Come, feast on it, my lord." The invitation made the lion angry. "I don't touch the flesh of the animal I have not killed," he growled.

The poor fox then went to a tiger and said "Sir, the lion has just killed an elephant. Now he has gone to take a bath, and I am guarding the flesh. Please come and enjoy it." But the tiger showed no interest and went away.

Finally, the fox approached a wolf and he agreed. As the wolf was eating, the lion happened to pass by. On seeing the lion, the wolf ran away. The fox, who had never really wanted to share his meal with anyone, happily ate the elephant.

3 The Tale of the Two Cats

A poor old woman once lived in a hut with a small thin cat. The cat lived on the measly leftovers and thin watery gruel that the old woman occasionally gave him.

One morning, the thin cat saw a fat cat walking along the wall of the opposite house. The thin cat called out to him, "My dear friend, it seems you get to feast everyday at a banquet. Pray, tell me where you find so much food."

The fat cat said, "At the king's table, of course. Every day, before the king sits down to eat, I hide under the table and steal the tasty pieces that drop from it."

The thin cat let out a long sigh of longing, and the fat cat said, "I can take you to the king's palace tomorrow. But remember, once we are there, you will have to fend for yourself."

"Oh thank you!" purred the thin cat joyfully, and he ran to tell his mistress.

The old woman was far from happy to hear him. "I beg you," she pleaded with her cat, "stay at home and be content with your gruel. What will happen if the royal servants catch you stealing?"

But the thin cat was so greedy that he paid no heed, and the two cats

started for the palace jauntily.

Now it had so happened that the day before, cats had invaded the king's banquet hall in such large numbers that the angry king had issued an order that any cat entering the palace gates would be put to death instantly. As the fat cat was creeping in through the gate, another cat, who was fleeing, warned him of the king's orders. The fat cat immediately turned and ran away.

But the thin cat was already close to the banquet hall. In a frenzy of excitement, he leapt through the window and was just snatching a piece of fish from a serving bowl, when a royal servant seized and killed him.

4 The Wild Boar and the Fox

A wild boar was whetting his tusks against a tree trunk. A fox saw him and wondered why the silly creature was preparing for a fight when there was no danger around. So he went up to the boar and asked, "Why are you whetting your tusks, dear friend? Look around. Is there any hunter or fierce animal? In fact, there is no danger at all. So I think what you are doing is totally useless."

The boar looked at him and remarked patiently, "O my dear friend! When danger arrives, it arrives suddenly. And when it comes, I may have something else in mind instead of whetting my tusks. As you know, it's too late to whet the sword when the trumpet for war blows."

5 The Foolish Raven

Once a raven saw a swan and, being all black himself, he was impressed with the bird's beautiful white colour. He longed to be as fair as the swan and thought if he lived in a pond like the swans do, he would become white too. So he left his usual haunt where he used to find his daily food and flew down to the pond. He plumed himself and washed his coat again and again. But all his efforts went in vain. His feathers remained as dark as they always were. The poor raven was doubly disappointed as he could not find his usual food in the new place. He soon died of hunger and grief.

Changing one's place of stay

6 The Miller Who Tried to Please Everyone

A miller and his son went to a country fair with their ass. On the way, they met some girls.

One of them said, "Look how foolish these two are. They have an ass, but they are walking beside it instead of riding it."

The father thought the girls were right and asked his son to ride the ass. Just then a good-natured fellow came up and offered a suggestion. He said that the ass looked weak and that instead of riding the animal, they should carry it on their shoulders." The miller agreed and thanked the man. He tied the legs of the ass and slung it across a long rod that he and his son could carry on their shoulders. They went along carrying the heavy load until they came to a large pool. While crossing over, they lost balance and fell into the water, ass and all.

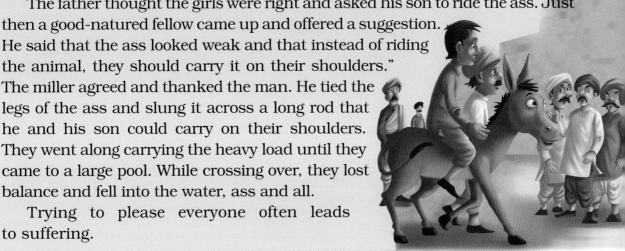

Trying to please everyone often leads to suffering.

7 The Wolf and the Pet Dog

A lean and hungry wolf once met a healthy pet dog. He was impressed with the dog's appearance and said, "Look at me, I'm hungry and weak. But you look well fed and full of energy. Where do you manage to get your food?"

The dog replied, "I watch over my master's house and they feed me in return."

"Is that so?" the wolf exclaimed. "Then I am ready to serve them too. I am sure they will feed me in exchange. Take me to your master, please. I need an easier life." The wolf paused for a moment and looked carefully at the dog. "What's that red mark on your neck, my friend?" he asked.

"Oh, it's nothing. They just put a chain on me so that I don't harm anyone or try to run away," the dog replied.

The wolf lost all his enthusiasm and said with a smile, "Farewell, friend. I'd rather perish a free creature than flourish as a slave."

8 The Hungry Dogs

There were three dogs who were very close friends. One day, the three dogs were very hungry as they had failed to find any food. Suddenly they saw some bones lying in the bottom of a stream. They tried hard to pick them up, but they were far below their reach. So they decided to drink up all the water of the stream and then get the bones. All three started drinking the water of the stream. After sometime, they felt full and their stomachs were bloated. But still they didn't stop drinking. Their stomachs grew bigger and bigger until they burst open and all the water gushed out. The three dogs now lay dead at the bottom of the stream.

If you attempt the impossible through foolish methods, you are bound to perish.

9 The Horse and the Ostler

A dishonest ostler used to steal the horse's oats and grains from the stable and take the booty to the market for sale. However, he always kept the horse clean, rubbed and polished his skin and took care of it so well that he looked very attractive and as fit as a fiddle. But the horse resented all the attention, for he knew the man's true nature. The ostler's motive for taking such good care of the horse was only too clear. One day, when the ostler was rubbing the horse, the horse said, "O man! If you really want me to look well, follow my simple instructions. Start feeding me more and grooming me less. Food will make me healthier, and then I'll no longer need the extra care to look well."

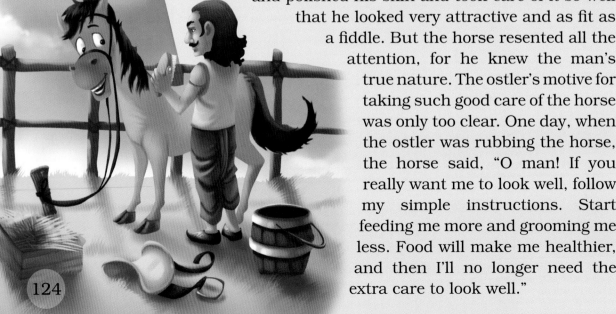

10 The Stag and the Ox

A stag rushed into a farmyard and took refuge in an ox stall to escape a pack of hounds. He covered himself with straw and said to the oxen, "Please let me hide here for some time. Some hounds are trying to catch me."

In the evening, the herdsman came into the stall to feed the cattle. He did not notice the stag and went away when his task was done. He was soon followed by a group of farmhands, and they too failed to notice. It was the end of the day and the stag felt relieved. "Oh friends," he said aloud. "I think I am out of danger now! I was here for so long and no one noticed me." Suddenly the master came in once more and called to one of his servants, "Why is the stall so unclean and why is there so little straw around?" he scolded. The servants immediately started cleaning the stall. They soon discovered the stag and seized it.

Nothing escapes the master's eyes.

11 The Fisherman and His Music

There was a fisherman who was more interested in exercising his musical talent than in tending to his fishing nets. One day, while casting his nets over the river, he started piping a beautiful tune. He thought the fish would be attracted and come into his nets. But to his disappointment, nothing of the sort happened. So he used baits and this time caught them in large numbers. But strangely, when he brought the fish ashore, they all started dancing. It was obvious they were dancing to appease him and win mercy. But the fisherman was hardly impressed. He said, "You did not dance when I played music for you. Now it hardly matters that you are trying to flatter me with your dancing."

The right thing should always be done at the right moment.

125

12 The Foolish Goat

One day a fox fell into a deep well. Soon a goat came up to the same well to take a drink. He was amazed to see a fox swimming in the water. The fox thought he must use the goat to rescue himself. He cried, "Hey, goat! Do you know why I am down in here? It's easiest to get all the good water if you are inside the well. Look! I am drinking and enjoying to my heart's content."

The fox's words tempted the goat, and he soon jumped into the well. The fox immediately caught hold of the goat, climbed onto his back, and after a little effort, managed to leap out of the well. The poor goat was almost drowning, and he cried out for help. The fox said, "You are a fool. Always look before you leap. Now that you have broken the golden rule, you deserve to suffer."

13 The Hart and the Hunters

Once upon a time, a hart was chased hard by a band of hunters. The poor creature hid himself behind a thick vine. The hunters searched all over but could not find him. So they went away. The hart thought the coast was clear and started browsing the vine in a relaxed way. One of the hunters heard the rustling sound and guessed where their prey was. He shot an arrow into the bush and it struck the hart. As he lay wreathing in agony, the hart said, "O poor me! I am an ungrateful creature and I deserve my plight. I injured the very plant that had protected me with its foliage. But now it is too late to make amends."

14 The Sick Hawk

Once upon a time, a hawk lived with his mother on the top of a tree. The son had a bad habit of stealing the religious offerings in the temples around. One day, the hawk fell sick and was nearing his death. He turned towards his weeping mother and said to her, "Mother, pray to the gods that they may take mercy on me and spare my life."

The mother replied, "O my foolish child! Which god can we pray to for mercy? Is there any whom you haven't outraged by robbing the offerings placed at their altars? After all your wrongdoings, how can you expect the gods would spare your life?"

Repentance on the deathbed does not suffice to make amends for the errors of a lifetime.

15 The Crow Who Wanted to Be a Peacock

A crow gathered together some peacock feathers one day and stuck them all over his body He was very proud of his new look and thought he should be living with peacocks instead of with crows. So he scoffed at his old friends and went and tried to mingle with a group of peacocks. However, the peacocks noticed in no time that there was a crow among them. They stripped him of all his colourful plumes, pecked at him and made fun of him. The bitter and battered crow returned home with a heavy heart. His fellow crows shook their heads and said, "You are a wretched creature! Had you been satisfied with your own feathers, you would never have had to face the taunts of your superiors or the hatred of your equals."

16 The Dog and the Hare

A dog and a hare happened to be very close friends. The hare was simple in nature while the dog was clever. One day the dog suddenly caught hold of the hare and bit him hard. The hare was in such pain that he thought he would die. The dog, however, started licking his wound as if he was trying to comfort the hare. The hare was confused at the dog's behaviour and did not know how to respond. He wondered what the dog really wanted. "Tell me first, are you a friend or an enemy? If you are a true friend, why did you bite me so hard? If you are an enemy, then why are you licking my wound? Either kill me or free me so that I can live a life of my own."

A dubious friend is worse than an enemy.

17 The Flies

One day a big jar full of honey fell from a high shelf on the kitchen floor and broke to pieces. The honey, which spilled out, attracted a swarm of flies. They sat and licked on it until they had finished it to the last drop. Having had their fill, they attempted to fly but failed as their feet had got stuck in the honey. They tried to fly again and again but all their efforts failed as they could not extricate their feet. They realized they were now in grave danger, as remaining on the kitchen floor they would sooner or later get noticed by humans and killed. One of them sighed in utter hopelessness, "Alas! How foolish we are! We risked our lives for a few moments of pleasure. Now we are about to die for our rashness and greed."

18 The Pig and the Sheep

There was a fat and healthy pig who was always scared to think he might be caught and slaughtered at any time. He took shelter in the sheepfold thinking it might help him avoid notice and escape the slaughterhouse. One day the shepherd saw him and grabbed him by his ear. The pig screamed and struggled with all his might to free himself from the man's clutches. A sheep who stood watching close by asked him to relax. "Why are you panicking? Our master does this often with us, but we don't cry like you. Stop the commotion," they said.

The pig replied, "My friend, my case is different. He catches hold of you to check or shear the wool. But men catch us to have delicious dinner."

19 The Sick Stag

An old stag fell so seriously ill that he could not move even to get his food. So he somehow dragged himself to a safe place where he could find greenery at hand. He was a warm and lovable creature and the other animals of the jungle came to see him from time to time. They all wished him to get well soon. But before leaving, many of them would eat the grass around him. As days passed, almost all the grass near him was eaten up. The stag recovered from his illness and, to his dismay, found the field around him was totally bare. He was weak still and could not move to the next field. The stag finally perished because of the insensitivity of his so-called friends.

129

20 The Lion and the Other Beasts

A lion once thought he would be able to hunt better if other animals helped him. So, one day, the lion formed a team with other beasts and with them managed to kill a fat stag. The lion came forward and said he would divide the stag's body into three parts for all to eat. Having done so, he took the biggest piece and said, "I take this for my role as the king of the jungle." Then he took another piece and said, "Now I take the second piece for taking part in hunting." Finally, pointing to the third piece, he said, "Look, here is the third piece. Anybody can take it from me if he dares." So the poor animals were left with nothing.

21 The Boys and the Frogs

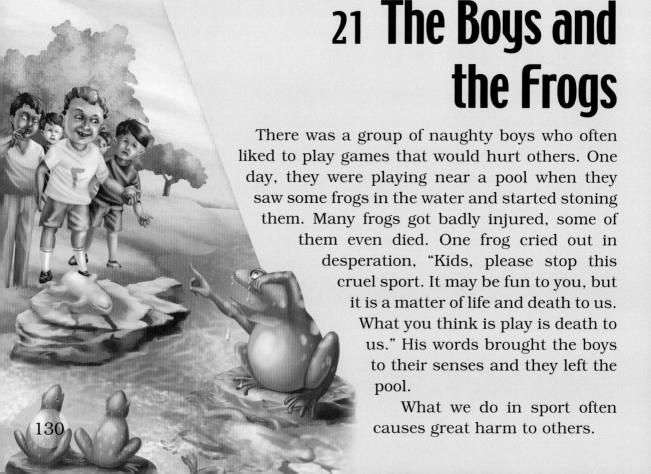

There was a group of naughty boys who often liked to play games that would hurt others. One day, they were playing near a pool when they saw some frogs in the water and started stoning them. Many frogs got badly injured, some of them even died. One frog cried out in desperation, "Kids, please stop this cruel sport. It may be fun to you, but it is a matter of life and death to us. What you think is play is death to us." His words brought the boys to their senses and they left the pool.

What we do in sport often causes great harm to others.

130

22 The Blacksmith and the Dog

There lived a blacksmith who had a pet dog. The dog used to sleep all through the day while his master was busy working. Even the sound of the hammer could not break his slumber. Every day he would wake up only after his master's working hours were over, for that was the time when the blacksmith would sit down for dinner. As his master ate, the dog would sit at his feet and wag his tail for titbits. One day, the blacksmith got angry and said, "You lazy laggard! You sleep all through the day even while I beat my hammer so loud. But you wake up at the sound of my teeth. Go away and leave me alone."

23 The Ass and the Statue

There was an ass who belonged to a man who made him toil very hard. The ass used to be whipped and lashed, so he did not find any occasion to feel happy about himself. One day, the ass was carrying the statue of a religious deity. He kept stopping on the road whenever devotees came forward to pay regards to the god. It was the festive season, and the ass thought all the devotion was meant for him. He stopped even more and started enjoying all the attention. His master, who was walking beside him, saw the ass's foolishness. He hit him hard with a stick and scolded him, saying, "Move on, you foolish beast. Do you think that these people are paying respect to you? It's only the statue you are carrying that has created a religious ardour. You are simply nothing."

Only fools take credit due to others.

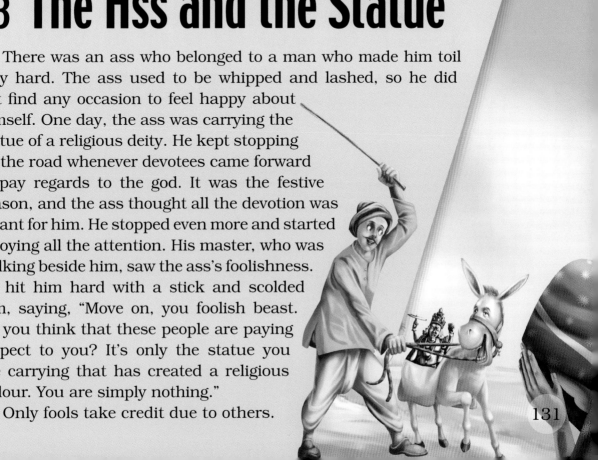

24 The Lion and the Farmer

A lion entered a farmyard and started prowling around for food. The farmer saw him and somehow locked the gate. The lion, seeing himself locked up, started killing all the cattle in a mad rage. The farmer now became scared for his own life. He quietly went up and opened the gate, and the lion escaped. The farmer was relieved, but he soon started lamenting over the huge damage to his property. His wife, who had watched everything from a distance, came up and tried to console him. "Don't cry, dear husband. Thank God you are alive. After all, it was your own mistake that caused all the havoc. What made you think you could punish a lion by locking him up in your home? If you had come across a lion in an open field, you would surely have run away."

It is better to scare away a thief than call harm upon yourself by trapping him.

25 The Lion and the Wolf

Once upon a time, a wolf killed a sheep and was about to carry the corpse to his den. Suddenly, a lion pounced forward and tried to snatch the sheep away. The wolf looked at the lion and shouted, "You should be ashamed of yourself. You are the king of the forest, and you know everyone trusts you. How can you rob me of my food? You are a disgrace to the forest!"

The lion laughed at the wolf and said, "Why should I be ashamed of myself? I have robbed someone who is a rogue himself and steals all the time. How dare you accuse me in this way, you wily beast. It is you who should be ashamed in the first place for having robbed the shepherd of his sheep."

One thief is no better than the other.

26 The Goat and the Goatherd

A goat stood on a huge rock, eating grass. He was so intent on his meal that he never once looked up at the other goats or the goatherd. As the flock moved away, the goatherd called and whistled for him again and again. But the goat was too busy eating and paid no heed. The goatherd lost his patience, picked up a stone and threw it at him. The stone struck the goat hard and broke one of his horns. Alarmed at the damage he had done, the goatherd ran up and begged him to keep the matter secret.

The goat smiled and said, "How foolish you are! Even if I don't speak a word, my broken horns will tell the entire story."

Facts speak plainer than words.

27 The Mouse and the Weasel

One day a greedy little mouse found a way to a farmer's storehouse and ate corns to his heart's content. By the time he finished eating, he had grown so fat that he could not make it through the very hole through which he had come in. He pushed hard, but his bloated body could not squeeze into the small opening. The mouse stood helpless, blaming his fate, when in came a weasel. He laughed at him and said, "Friend, take my advice. There is only one way to get out of the storehouse. Wait here until you grow lean and hungry again. Then you will see how easy it is to pass through the hole. Stop eating and you will find out for yourself." And that was all the sympathy the poor mouse got.

Greediness leads to nothing but sorrow.

28 The Lion and the Three Councillors

A lion had the habit of consulting other animals of the forest on trivial matters. One day, he called a sheep to him and asked whether there was any smell in his breath. The sheep replied, "Yes." The lion was angry with his blunt reply and bit off his head for being a fool. He then asked the wolf the same question. The wolf wanted to play safe and said, "No." The lion saw that he was lying and killed him too. Finally he called the fox and repeated his question. The fox was wise and decided to avoid any kind of risk whatsoever. He said, "Apologies, my dear lord, but I cannot answer your question. The fact is, I have caught cold and can't smell at all."

29 The Sick Lion

An old lion fell ill and could not move. He sent word across the forest about his poor condition. The animals were all sorry for him and started visiting him one by one. But the news was in reality a trap laid by the sick lion. When the unsuspecting animals came to see him, he caught and ate them one by one. One day it was the turn of the fox to visit the lion. The fox was wise; he entered the lion's cave and stood at a safe distance. The lion called him closer, but the fox stood in his place and said, "Sorry, sir, I am safe where I am. I see footprints of other animals coming into the cave. But there is not a single one going out."

You should not enter into a risk unless you know the way out.

30 The Farmer and the Dogs

It was a snowy winter day and a farmer was sitting hungry in his home as it was too cold to go out for food. Soon he was so desperate with hunger that he started eating his own cattle. Days passed, but outside it continued to snow. Having finished off the cattle, the farmer now started consuming his sheep. A few more days went by, but still the weather remained as bad as before. At last he turned to the oxen and ate them one by one. The farmer had some dogs too, and they quietly watched the farmer's activities. One day, they said to each other, "Let's get out of the place. Our master has no pity for any of us. He did not even spare the oxen who carry so much burden for him. Once the oxen are eaten, he would surely make us his next meal."

If our neighbour's house is on fire, we should take measures to save ourselves.

31 The Big Fish

A small pond was inhabited by fish of all sizes. All the fish, big and small, lived together in perfect peace and harmony. One day, a fisherman cast his net into the pond. When he drew it up, he was amazed to see the variety of his catch. As he was taking out the huge haul from the net, most of the small fish managed to escape through holes in the net and jumped back into the deep water. The big fish had no option but to stay in the net as they could hardly move their weight in the net. They were thrown into the boat and soon killed by the fisherman.

It is not smart or safe for big fish to stay in small ponds.

135

1 The Story of the Merchant's Son

A merchant's son purchased a book for Rs.100. It had just one sentence, 'Man gets what he is destined to'. The merchant was annoyed at his foolishness and threw him out of his house. The poor boy went to another city and began a new life under the name Prapta.

Chandravati, the princess of the city, loved a handsome warrior and asked her maid to arrange a meeting with him. The maid secretly invited the warrior to the palace that night. She asked him to climb the palace wall with the help of a rope that would be hanging there.

The warrior, however, was not interested in meeting the princess and never turned up. Meanwhile, Prapta noticed the suspended rope, climbed the wall and found himself in the princess' bedroom.

The princess, mistaking him for the warrior, said to him, "O handsome soldier, I have fallen in love with you." To this Prapta replied, "Man gets what he is destined to."

The princess realized this man was not the one she was expecting, and she asked him to go away. Prapta left the palace and went to sleep at a temple. But the Mayor of the city had come to hold a secret meeting there and told Prapta to sleep at his house.

When Prapta reached the Mayor's house, his daughter Vinayawati mistook him for her prospective husband and made arrangements to marry him. Before tying the knot, Vinayawati asked Prapta to say something, and he recited his usual sentence about destiny. His words annoyed her and she asked him to leave at once.

Prapta once again took to the street. His eyes fell on a marriage procession in which an elephant had gone berserk and was charging at everyone. The bridegroom and his party soon fled the scene of marriage.

Prapta saw that the frightened bride was alone. He came forward and drove away the elephant courageously. Meanwhile, as peace returned, the bride's father, a merchant, along with the marriage party, came back to the venue. The daughter told her father, "This brave man saved me from the mad elephant. I won't marry anyone but him."

Hearing the commotion, the princess and the king came to the wedding venue to see what had happened, and so did the Mayor's daughter. The king asked Prapta to tell him everything without fear. Prapta as usual repeated the same sentence.

The sentence rang a bell in the princess' head. The Mayor's daughter was also reminded of her meeting with Prapta. The king, the Mayor, and the merchant, all three married off their daughters to Prapta and the king gave him a thousand villages as a wedding gift. Everyone agreed that even God cannot undo what is destined for man.

2 The Greedy Little Bird

Long ago on a hot summer day the king of birds, along with other birds, flew to a new place in search of food. He asked them to begin searching in all directions.

All the birds flew far and wide in search of food. One of the birds reached a highway. There she saw many bullock carts carrying sacks of food grains. She also noticed that lots of grains were falling on the road as the carts moved.

She was delighted and decided to tell the king about this place before anyone else found it. So she flew back and said to the king of birds, "I saw a place where many sack-laden bullock carts pass by on the road and spill grains. But if you fly down on that road to peck at the grain, the carts may crush you at any time. It's better not to go there at all."

The bird's advice seemed sensible and the king agreed. He warned the other birds not to go anywhere near the highway.

The little bird would secretly fly to the spot everyday and enjoy the feast alone. One day, while she was pecking at the grains, a bullock cart came up and crushed the greedy bird.

3 The Merchant and the Pawnbroker

A poor merchant asked a pawnbroker to keep his weighing scales. After a few weeks, he asked for his scales back. The pawnbroker said, "Oh, the mice ate it, my friend!"

The merchant decided to teach him a lesson and said, "I want to have a bath in the river. Can I take your son along?"

The pawnbroker agreed. When the duo reached the banks of the river, the merchant locked the boy in a hut nearby. Seeing him return alone, the pawnbroker asked about his son. The merchant replied, "A big hawk has snatched him away!"

"How can a hawk carry away such a big boy?" asked the furious pawnbroker.

"If mice can eat an iron weighing scale, then a hawk can surely carry away a boy!" the merchant replied.

The pawnbroker at once returned the scales. The merchant released his son.

4 The Old Woman and Her Son

There lived a mother and a son who loved each other very much. Their mutual adoration made the son's wife very jealous. She felt that her husband loved his mother more than he loved her and planned to throw her mother-in-law out of the house. After much effort, she finally succeeded in doing so.

The old mother had no option but to start living alone. Time passed and a child was born to the young couple. News reached the old woman and she longed to see and bless the child. But the wife didn't allow her entry. The old woman broke down and went to a temple to complain to God. God, moved by her grief, came down to earth and rebuked her daughter-in-law. The latter then realized her mistake and reunited the old woman with her son.

5 The Miser

There once lived a miser who sold all his worldly possessions in exchange of a huge lump of gold. He hid it in a hole behind his house and kept visiting the spot frequently to make sure it was safe. His behaviour raised the curiosity of one of his servants. One day when the miser was absent, he peeped into the hole and discovered the shining lump of gold. Some time later, the miser returned and found that the hole was empty. He fell to the ground and started crying in despair. His neighbour came running to him and said, "Stop crying, my friend, and put a stone in that hole. After all, you never meant to sell the gold. It was just a precious object you liked to admire. It had no use for anyone. A stone in its place will hardly make any difference."

6 The Lion and the Mouse

It was a warm day and a lion was taking a nap in his cave. Suddenly a mouse ran over his nose by mistake and awakened the great beast. The lion was about to crush the mouse under his paws, when the little creature started begging for his life. The lion took pity on the mouse and let it go. A few days later, the lion, while wandering in the forest, stepped into a trap set by hunters and was caught in the nets. He was so tightly entangled in ropes that he could hardly move. The lion lay on the ground and roared helplessly. His cries echoed across the forest and reached the mouse's ears. He rushed to the spot and bit the threads of the net into pieces.

At times even the small and the weak turn out to be mightier than most.

141

7 The Hare and the Hound

One day a hound scared a hare out of its burrow and chased it for a long distance. The hare, thanks to its speed and agility, soon went far out of the reach of the dog. The dog stopped trailing and turned to go back. A man passing by witnessed the whole incident. He laughed at the bulky hound and mocked him, saying, "You lazy laggard. You could not even catch a tiny, weak, little hare! Shame on you! What else is your speed meant for then?" The hound turned towards the man and replied, "You are getting it wrong, my friend. I was only chasing it for a delicious dinner. But the hare was running for its life."

8 The Herdsman

A herdsman found one of his calves missing and went searching for it at once. As he looked for it everywhere, he prayed to the deities of the forest and vowed to sacrifice a lamb if he found the calf. Suddenly, as he approached the cliff, he saw a lion eating the little creature he was looking for. It struck the herdsman that the beast might catch him as well and he started running for his life. He was so scared that as he ran he once again started praying to the gods. This time he promised he would sacrifice a bull if they saved him from the lion. The gods, as usual, remained silent.

If all such rash vows were to be granted, most men would be ruined by their own words.

9 The Nurse and the Wolf

A hungry wolf was passing by a hut when he heard a nurse scolding a crying baby. "Come on, baby, that's enough! If you don't stop crying now, I'll put you outside the house and the wolf will come and take you away." The hungry wolf thought this was the easiest way to get food. If the child did not stop crying, he would be the gainer and get to eat his tender flesh.

So he sat there and waited and waited till it was dusk. He heard the nurse speaking once more. But this time she said, "O sweet baby! If the naughty wolf comes near you, I will beat him to death."

The wolf was shocked, He realized that human beings should never be trusted as they were never serious about their own words and made false

10 The Pearl String

A queen asked her maid to keep her pearl necklace safe with her while she went for a bath in the river. But the maid fell fast asleep, and a monkey, seeing the necklace lying beside her, ran away with it. The maid woke up and found the pearls missing. She immediately raised an alarm and informed the intelligent chief guard. He guessed it must be the work of a monkey and thought of a trick to catch it. He brought several strings of glass beads and hung them on the bushes all around. All the monkeys, except the culprit, started picking up the pretty strings and dancing around in joy. Then the rogue monkey came down and declared proudly, "You have strings of glass beads, but I have one of pearls!"

The chief guard, who was waiting for this moment, caught the monkey and got him to give back the pearl string.

Boasting can often lead us to ruin.

143

11 The Woodcutter and the Trees

A poor woodcutter knelt down beneath the tallest tree and prayed for a new handle for his saw. He kept on praying and pleading till the trees took pity on him. The chief of the trees declared that the ash tree was best suited for the woodcutter's purpose and asked it to speak to him. The woodcutter followed the ash tree's instructions and made a new handle out of its wood that fitted perfectly with his axe. The woodcutter was thrilled and thought this was an opportunity to make money by gathering more wood for such articles of use. He immediately started chopping at the trees around him. The chief of the trees realized his mistake and said, "O poor ash tree, I sacrificed you for the sake of this selfish man. And now we are on the verge of extinction."

The rich harm the poor but end up as losers.

12 The Lion and the Fox

A lion, a fox and an ass went out for hunting. As they roamed the forest, they came across a big stag. Together they gave it a chase, killed it and then decided to divide the meal. The ass came forward and divided the heap of flesh into three portions. The lion, however, was furious as he wanted the biggest share. He pounced on the ass and killed him instantly. Then the lion asked the fox to divide the meat. The fox was wise. He gathered every piece in a heap, separated a tiny amount from it and set it aside for himself. The lion, quite amused, asked him, "Who taught you this art of division?"

The fox wittily replied, "Sir, the ass's fate!"

It is better to learn from the mistakes of others than from your own.

13 The Nymph and the Ascetic

The Bodhisattva was born into a rich family. When he grew up, he renounced all worldly pleasures and became an ascetic. One morning, when he was meditating near a river, a water nymph caught sight of him and fell in love. "A handsome man like him doesn't deserve to lead a life of hardship," the nymph said to herself. She started singing a beautiful song hoping to attract the Bodhisattva's attention. But the Bodhisattva continued to sit still with his eyes closed. Surprised, the nymph went up to him and said, "O, my lord! Why not keep your meditations for your old age? Right now you are too young for such hardship." The ascetic opened his eyes, smiled and said, "My dear good lady, I do not know whether I will live that long." The nymph realized that she would never be able to win him over and vanished forever.

14 The Milkmaid

There once lived a milkmaid in a village. She used to daydream about becoming a rich lady one day. Once, when she was going to sell milk to the market with the pail on her head, she began to daydream again.

"I'll sell the milk at a good price today," she thought, very pleased with herself.

"And then with that money, I'll buy some nice hens," she continued dreaming. "The hens will lay eggs everyday. Then I'll sell milk and eggs everyday, and then more milk and more eggs, for I'll keep buying new cows and hens for my farm."

All this while, the milkmaid was paying no attention to where she was going.

"I'll make a lot of money soon, then I'll buy beautiful new dresses and everyone will praise my beauty. But I'll just toss my head and take no notice of them!" And saying so she tossed her head and the milk pail fell down, spilling all the milk on the ground.

Because of her dreaming, the milkmaid was now left with nothing to sell in reality.

15 A Mountain in Labour

Many years ago, a mighty rumbling sound was heard from a mountain. It created a huge curiosity among the villagers. They all rushed to a spot from where they could watch what was happening. Many of them said that the mountain must be in labour. Everyone held their breath in suspense and listened as the sound increased. As the mountain trembled and roared, they started wondering what it was giving birth to. Some said it might be another mountain, or a big solid rock. The villagers stood and waited, but none had a clear idea of what was really going on. Suddenly, much to their shock, out popped a tiny mouse from the crater.

A grand beginning does not always lead to a grand ending.

16 The Mask

A fox was wandering the city streets when he decided to investigate an actor's house. He slipped into one of the rooms and started playing with the things that lay there. Among the many curiosities, he hit upon a mask. He was amazed at its beauty. "Ah! What a fine thing," he said to himself. He liked the mask so much that he decided to wear it and see how he looked. He said, "If I wear it, I can easily pretend to have a human head. It's beautiful." He put it on and came to a mirror to see his reflection. "How beautiful and intelligent I look now! This is really impressive. But it makes me sad to think that this human head has no human brain behind it."

Beauty without brain is really next to nothing.

17 The Bull and the Goat

Once a lion was prowling through the forest when he caught sight of a bull and started chasing it. The bull ran as fast as he could and took refuge in a dugout which was the home of a goat. The goat was not at all happy to receive the unwanted visitor and got into a fight. He tried to push out the bull by hitting him with his horns again and again. The bull put up with the assaults patiently, and said to the fuming goat, "I will not fight back now, but don't suppose I am afraid of you. What I am really scared of is the lion waiting outside this shelter. Once the lion goes away, I will show you the difference between a bull and a goat." The goat came to his senses and stopped fighting.

One should never approach mean people when one is in distress.

18 The One-eyed Doe

A one-eyed doe used to graze near the seaside. She knew she had to be constantly on the alert to save herself from any sudden attacks from hunters. So, she always kept an eye on the surrounding fields presuming that the hunters would come by that route. She never watched the sea, as it didn't occur to her that hunters could approach through the water. One day, some men came rowing by in a boat. Seeing the doe grazing there, they aimed their arrows at her, and in no time she was shot to the ground. The doe, heaving her last breath, said to herself, "How strange are the ways of destiny! I thought the land was dangerous. But my enemy gave me the death blow from the side I thought was safe."

Danger often comes from the source least suspected.

19 The Woodcutter and the Fox

A fox, chased by hunters, rushed to a woodcutter and begged for shelter. The woodcutter pointed his finger at his hut and the fox took refuge there. The hunters soon came up and asked, "Have you seen a fox around?"

The woodcutter said, "No," but silently pointed his finger to the corner of the hut. The hunters did not understand the hint and left. The fox readily jumped out of the hut and started running away. The hunter called to him and said, "How ungrateful you are! You haven't even thanked me for saving your life!"

The fox replied curtly, "I would have thanked you had your actions been as trustworthy as your words."

A wink sometimes is more malicious than words.

20 The Monkey and the Camel

Many years ago, all the animals of the forest assembled together in a show of their histrionic talents. As the audience waited, the monkey was asked to dance. Known for his natural acrobatic skills, the monkey delighted everyone with his moves. There was a huge applause and the monkey was hailed as a great dancer. The camel could not stand all that praise. He jumped up and started dancing too. But his performance had neither rhythm nor grace and he ended up making a fool of himself. As a punishment for his jealousy, he was banished from the land.

If you stretch your arms beyond your sleeves, you are bound to suffer.

21 The Ass and the Lapdog

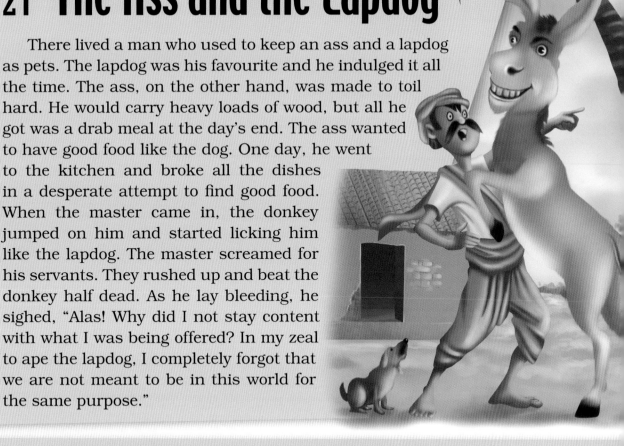

There lived a man who used to keep an ass and a lapdog as pets. The lapdog was his favourite and he indulged it all the time. The ass, on the other hand, was made to toil hard. He would carry heavy loads of wood, but all he got was a drab meal at the day's end. The ass wanted to have good food like the dog. One day, he went to the kitchen and broke all the dishes in a desperate attempt to find good food. When the master came in, the donkey jumped on him and started licking him like the lapdog. The master screamed for his servants. They rushed up and beat the donkey half dead. As he lay bleeding, he sighed, "Alas! Why did I not stay content with what I was being offered? In my zeal to ape the lapdog, I completely forgot that we are not meant to be in this world for the same purpose."

22 The Hares and the Frogs

A group of hares was facing continual threat to their lives as there were hunters all around their home. One day they decided that they would commit mass suicide as living in fear was worse than death itself. Together they went towards a lake to drown themselves. It was night and the

moon shone brightly. A number of frogs were playing in the pleasant breeze near the lake. Hearing the footsteps of the hares, they all panicked and jumped back into the water. An elderly hare stopped the procession and said, "Brothers, why not think again? It's true that we suffer all the time. But having seen how easily these frogs get scared, I now feel we are certainly not the worst sufferers." The rest of the hares were moved by his wisdom and returned home.

23 The Little Fish

A fisherman once caught only one little fish after a daylong wait. The fish pleaded, "O fisherman! Spare me my life. I'm but a small catch and hardly worth a meal. If you release me in the water, I'll grow bigger and then you can catch me once more." The fisherman laughed out loudly at his ridiculous promise. "My dear friend, how can I believe your words?" he said. "If I let you go this time, you'll never come under my net again. Once you grow up, it will be easier for you to make out a trap, and you'll escape me always. I'm not so foolish as to throw away my small catch in the hope of a bigger one that may never come my way." He put the poor fish in his bag and went home.

24 The Goat and the Ox

There was a farmer who had a goat and an ox. Unlike the ox, the goat had never felt the yoke on his neck and was used to running around freely in the field. He made fun of the poor ox for meekly submitting to the yoke and for toiling all through the day. The ox kept silent and concentrated upon his work. Soon it was time for a religious festival. The farmer caught hold of the goat and started dragging him to the altar for sacrifice. The ox stood in the crowd, and as the goat passed, he said to him, "Your idleness has led you to this situation, my friend. I must say that in spite of all my suffering and my heavy toil, I'm luckier than you. You enjoyed free time and spent your days basking in the sun. You neither worked nor bore the weight of the yoke. But at the end of the day, I have survived, not you."

25 The Mice and the Cat

Once there were some mice who were fed up with the constant attacks of a cat living nearby. So, they decided to figure out a way to solve the problem once and for all. They met and hit upon a plan to watch the cat and track his movements. "Let's put a bell around his neck," suggested a mouse who was wiser than the rest. "It will help us know where he goes."

"Done," said everyone. "This is the best plan." There was a huge round of applause for the brilliant idea. But among them was a small old mouse who sat still and shook his head. "O friends! I've a small question," he began, and everyone looked at him. "Who among you would be willing to hang the bell around the cat's neck?" he asked.

The mice were all silent for none could answer that question.

26 The Hunter

There was a hunter who made a living by selling birds. He was an honest man, although his profession involved catching and killing innocent creatures. One day, he caught a partridge in his net, and the little bird started pleading for his life. "Please let me go. Spare my poor life," he begged. "I promise I will come to your aid whenever you need. If you want, I will send a decoy bird and lead other birds to you so that you can catch them instead."

The falconer listened to him patiently and said, "I had thought I would release you. But I can see there is a traitor in you. You care nothing about killing your brothers for the sake of your own life. You deserve a punishment that is worse than death."

151

27 The Rivers and the Sea

Since olden times the rivers and the seas lived in perfect harmony. The rivers would pour all their water into the sea, and the sea would happily accept it so that the rivers remained clean and safe. The rivers, however, were not happy with the fact that the sea turned all the water salty. One day, they decided to make a complaint, They joined in one body and moved towards the sea. When they reached the vast blue expanse, they asked all in one voice, "O sea, why is it that you always make salty the sweet water we pour into you everyday?"

The sea remained unmoved by all this collective anger and replied calmly, "If you do not wish to become salty, keep away from me."

The rivers returned crestfallen, as they knew they could not do without the sea.

28 Proud Padanjali

Brahmadatta, the king of Benaras, had a son named Padanjali. The prince, a good-for-nothing brat, spent his days idling around. The king was worried the boy's behaviour was not in any way fit for a royal person destined to sit on the throne. The king, however, failed to bring him back on the right path and died a troubled man. The Bodhisattva, who was the chief minister, decided to test prince Padanjali before crowning him the king. He publicly asked the prince to give an account of the duties and responsibilities of a ruler. The vain prince could not give a proper reply and failed to mention anything about the welfare of the people. The word soon spread that Padanjali lacked the qualities of a ruler and was unfit to be the king. Finally the Bodhisattva received the crown instead of Padanjali.

29 The Righteous King

The Bodhisattva was the king of a prosperous kingdom. However, as time passed, untimely deaths began plaguing his empire. He called an urgent meeting of his ministers and priests, and asked them the reason for all the suffering.

"My Lord, it seems the gods are unhappy with us!" suggested a minister.

"If that is the case, then we must organise a grand ritual and sacrifice a hundred lambs to appease them," responded the head priest.Everybody, except the king, welcomed this idea.

"I do not want to bring happiness to my kingdom by slaughtering animals!" the king protested. "Only with peace, love and a righteous rule will I appease the gods!"

The Bodhisattva was right. He kept working hard for the well-being of all his subjects, and within a few days, the diseases and untimely deaths ceased.

30 The Shepherd and the Sea

There once lived a shepherd who decided to spend his life sailing. So, one day, he sold his flock, purchased a cargo of dates, and set out on his voyage. He did not sail far when a violent storm came and made the calm, placid ocean all violent. The cargo could not take the force of huge waves and fell into the water. The shepherd, however, managed to survive the storm and swim back to the shore. When he reached land, the sea was calm again. A friend came and joined him as he stood gazing miserably at the sea. As they started walking together, the friend said that the calmness and beauty of the waters was really inviting. The shepherd, by now the wiser for his experience, said, "Look carefully, my friend. The calmness is only meant for us to find the lost dates."

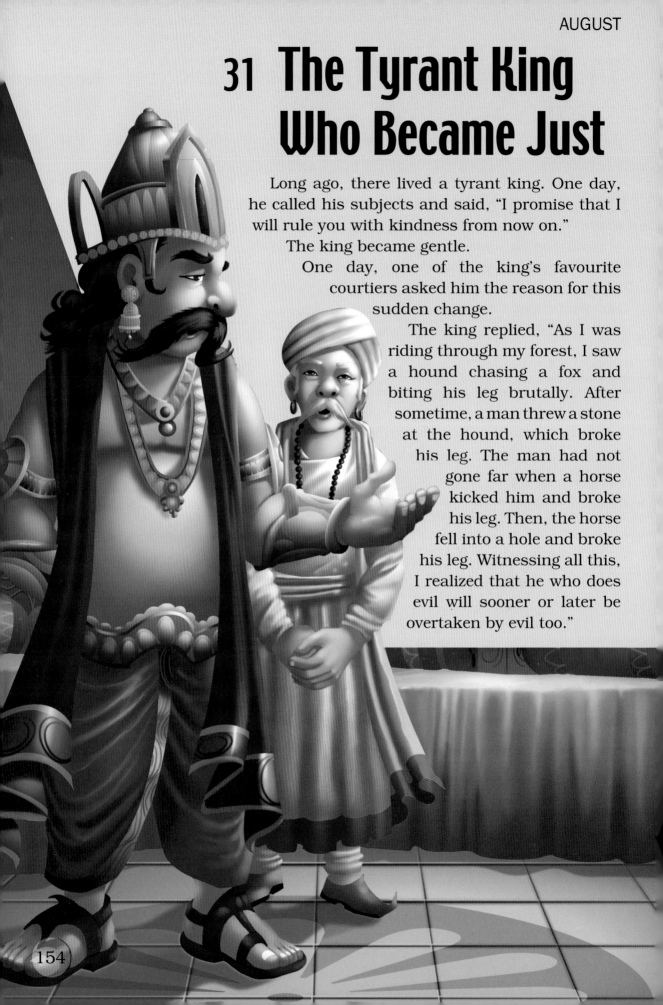

31 The Tyrant King Who Became Just

Long ago, there lived a tyrant king. One day, he called his subjects and said, "I promise that I will rule you with kindness from now on."

The king became gentle.

One day, one of the king's favourite courtiers asked him the reason for this sudden change.

The king replied, "As I was riding through my forest, I saw a hound chasing a fox and biting his leg brutally. After sometime, a man threw a stone at the hound, which broke his leg. The man had not gone far when a horse kicked him and broke his leg. Then, the horse fell into a hole and broke his leg. Witnessing all this, I realized that he who does evil will sooner or later be overtaken by evil too."

1 The Merchant, the Monk and the Barber

There was a merchant who lost his entire fortune. One night, a Jain monk appeared in his dream and said, "I am wealth. Tomorrow morning, I shall come to your home. Strike me on the head with a stick, and I shall turn into gold. After that, you will never be poor again."

Next morning, a Jain monk appeared in the doorway. He was a spitting image of the one that the merchant had seen in his dream. When the merchant saw him, he was delighted, and immediately struck him on his head with a stout stick. The monk fell to the ground and turned into a pile of gold. The merchant picked up the gold and quietly hid it in a secluded room of the house.

However, a barber had witnessed this entire occurrence. When he reached home, he thought, "If these Jain monks turn into gold when hit on the head, why shouldn't I invite a few of them to my house?"

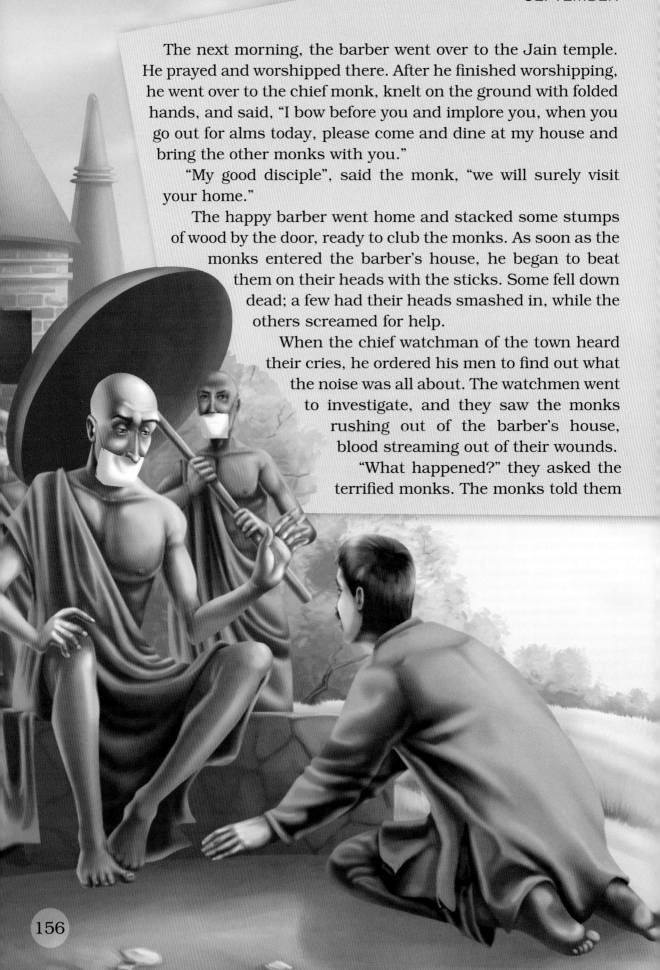

The next morning, the barber went over to the Jain temple. He prayed and worshipped there. After he finished worshipping, he went over to the chief monk, knelt on the ground with folded hands, and said, "I bow before you and implore you, when you go out for alms today, please come and dine at my house and bring the other monks with you."

"My good disciple", said the monk, "we will surely visit your home."

The happy barber went home and stacked some stumps of wood by the door, ready to club the monks. As soon as the monks entered the barber's house, he began to beat them on their heads with the sticks. Some fell down dead; a few had their heads smashed in, while the others screamed for help.

When the chief watchman of the town heard their cries, he ordered his men to find out what the noise was all about. The watchmen went to investigate, and they saw the monks rushing out of the barber's house, blood streaming out of their wounds.

"What happened?" they asked the terrified monks. The monks told them what the barber had done. The watchmen arrested the barber at once and took him and the wounded monks to the court of law.

In court, the judges asked the barber, "Why did you commit this wicked crime?"

"It wasn't my fault", he lamented. "I saw a merchant do the same and thought I would try too." He told them what that he had witnessed at the merchant's house. The judges immediately ordered the merchant to appear before them, and asked him, "Have you been killing any monks?"

The merchant told them about the monk in his dream. The judges said, "Let this barber, who blindly imitated the merchant, be put to death."

The very next day, the barber was hanged.

2 The Old Tiger and the Greedy Traveller

An old tiger found he no longer had the strength to hunt for food. Holding a golden bracelet, he stood in the mud and started shouting, "Look, everyone! Come and take this beautiful piece of gold jewellery."

A passerby felt tempted, but was also scared to approach a tiger. "How can I trust you?" he asked from a safe distance. "You may eat me up if I try to take that bracelet."

The tiger replied, "I used to kill others. But now I lead a pious life and enjoy giving." The traveller came up to the tiger, but he got stuck in the mud. The old tiger had been waiting for this moment. He pounced on him and started dragging him through the mud. The man lamented, "Oh poor me! In my greed, I forgot the simple rule that a killer always remains a killer."

3 The Crow and the Quail

A crow and a quail were very good friends. One day they set off to attend an invitation from a common friend. On the way, they came across a cowherd who was carrying a pot full of curd on his head. The crow could not resist the temptation and started pecking at the pot. As the pot shook, the cowherd got annoyed and stopped to look around. The crow sensed danger and flew away fast. The cowherd noticed a quail flying over his pot. He thought that the quail was trying to get at the curd and killed it with a stone. The poor quail thus lost his life for having kept bad company.

4 The Frog and the Mouse

A wicked frog once made friends with a mouse. One day they set out on a long journey. On the way, they came across a pond. The mouse was scared of entering the water, but the frog assured the mouse he would help him cross the pond. He tied the legs of the mouse with his own legs and took a plunge in the water. As the frog reached the middle of the pond, where the water was deepest, he started dragging the mouse below the water. The mouse struggled hard to free himself, and their tussle created a huge commotion in the water. The disturbance attracted the attention of a hawk hovering over the pond. It flew down, snatched up the mouse in its talons and flew away. The treacherous frog suffered along with the mouse as his legs were tied to the mouse and he was taken away too.

Those who harm others often become victims of their own actions.

159

5 The Hen and the Cat

Once upon a time there was a clever hen. One day, the hen fell ill and was lying in her nest when a cat came to see her. He crept into her nest and said, "My dear friend, how are you? May I help you in any way? I will fetch you whatever you want. Is there anything I can get you right now?"

The hen listened to his over-friendly words and sensed danger. She said, "Yes, of course. Do me a favour, please. Leave my place. I am sick, and I don't want to run into more trouble by allowing in an unwanted guest."

6 The Mule

A mule was born out of wedlock between an ass and a horse. The little mule took lots of corn every day and soon grew strong and healthy. He loved frisking about and running in the sun. He was so full of energy that he thought, "My mother must have been a thoroughbred racer. But I am faster than her. I must see how far I can run."

He started running hard but soon felt that he could not make it very far. He was thoroughly exhausted and, as he came to a halt, he remembered the hard truth about himself. It was that even though his mother was a horse, his father was none other than a mere ass. The mule realized that his energy had its limits and that he could never run as fast as a horse.

Every situation has two sides, a good and a bad, and you should understand both in order to lead a balanced life.

7 The Stallion and the Poor Ass

A proud stallion was on his way to the battlefield when he came upon an ass crossing the road. The sight of the bulky animal blocking his way threw the stallion into a temper. "Move away from my path right now, you stupid beast, or I will trample you," he shouted. The ass felt insulted but said nothing and gently moved towards the other side of the road. A few days later, the ass met the same stallion walking down the same road. Things had changed since the first time they met. The war was over and the stallion's noble, caring master was dead. The stallion himself was wounded, lame and almost blind. He was carrying a heavy load and was being whipped mercilessly by his new master.

The path of contempt does not lead to glory.

8 The Old Lady and Her Maids

Once there was a thrifty old lady who used to keep two maid servants in her house. She had the curious habit of calling them to work at the crack of dawn when her pet cock started crowing. The maids never liked to wake up so early and they decided to kill the cock. They thought once the crowing stopped they would be able to sleep more. They secretly killed the bird, but the act got them into more trouble. The old woman was now scared that without the cock she might oversleep. She started getting up at odd hours all through the night and issuing orders. The maids regretted having killed the cock, but it was too late for amends.

Too much cunning can undermine its very purpose.

9 The Sensible Enemy

A prince and his two friends climbed a hill and found many precious stones lying around. One of the three said, "It's not safe to go back carrying these stones. But we cannot leave them here either. So let's swallow them and go home." The rest agreed.

A thief overheard their plans, came up, and made friends with them. The boys swallowed the stones and were returning home with their new friend when they were caught by a gang of bandits. The bandits felt sure they were carrying good money and searched them thoroughly. But they did not find anything, so they threatened to cut open their stomachs.

The thief thought, "I'll not let these boys die for no reason."

He came forward and offered himself to be put under the knife first. His stomach was slashed but nothing precious was found. The bandits thought there was no use in cutting up the three boys, as it might just turn out to be a waste of time. So while the thief lay bleeding to death, the boys were released.

Sometimes even a thief can have a golden heart.

10 The Naïve Farmer

One day a devastating flood washed away all the crops in a field, leaving the villagers in deep trouble. A farmer went to the village headman for help, and the latter gave him an ox to plough the field. The headman happened to have a secret understanding with the farmer's wife. The farmer soon grew suspicious that the two were up to something. He planned to catch them red-handed and made a false show that he was going abroad.

The headman, thinking that the farmer was away, came to meet the wife. But as they were about to close the door, the farmer suddenly appeared. Seeing him, they started putting up an act as if they did not know each other. But this time they could not fool the farmer. He bashed up the headman and gave his wife a sound scolding.

Treachery never pays.

11 The Lion and the Bear

One day a lion and a bear both saw a fawn and pounced on it at the same time. As neither of them was ready to let the other one get away with the prey, a long gruelling fight between the two heavyweights started. After some time, they both injured themselves and lay half dead on the ground. A fox, who was roaming nearby, had stood and witnessed the entire drama. He stealthily stepped between them and quietly carried away the dead fawn. When they discovered the loss, the lion said sadly, "How foolish we have been. We fought with each other only to serve a rogue a delicious dinner. Shame on us!"

Sometimes one man's toil is another man's profit.

12 The Valuer and His Nose

A king had a greedy valuer who used to examine swords and fix their worth. He used to set high prices for the swords of those dealers who secretly offered him bribes. While valuing swords, the man would always smell the blade and give an impression that his value was above all judgement.

One day a talented craftsman offered his sword for valuation without bribing the valuer. The valuer smelled and rejected the sword saying it was of bad quality.

The craftsman knew the valuer was lying and approached the king. This time he secretly smeared the sword with chili powder. The king ordered the valuer to check the sword once more. The valuer smelled the blade and the chili powder passed into his nose. He jumped up and sneezed with all his might. The sword slipped from his hand, fell on his nose and cut it off.

Thus the valuer was punished for his greed.

13 The Peach and the Apple

One day a peach and an apple were having an argument in an orchard. Each was trying to prove that he was more beautiful than the other. As none seemed to win, they decided to settle the issue through an open debate. A loud exchange of words began again between the two fruits while other fruits listened. A blackberry in the nearby bush thrust its head out and cried, "Your dispute has gone on long enough and does not seem to settle. There is nothing that you will gain from it. So forget your differences, shake hands and be friends again. This is the only way to live in peace."

Loudest quarrels are often the pettiest ones.

14 The Bald Knight

A knight was losing his hair as he was growing old. One day, to his utter dismay, he found he was completely bald. He was angry and frustrated, but he knew he had to accept the inevitable. He decided he would hide his baldness and started using a wig. One day he went out for hunting with his friends. While he was roaming the forest in search of wild animals, a sudden gusty wind blew his wig away. His companions were amazed to see his bald head, and they all laughed out loudly. At first the knight was a little disconcerted, but soon he too burst into laughter. "How silly I am," he said, laughing. "How can I expect a wig to stay on my head when my own hair could not?"

15 Canda and the King of Benaras

The Bodhisattva was married to a beautiful girl called Canda. One day, while they were frolicking in a stream, King Brahmadatta of Benaras saw Canda and fell in love with her. Taking the man beside her to be her husband, the king shot him dead with his arrow.

He thought that, with her husband dead, the girl would surely agree to marry him. After all he was a mighty king. As Canda sat wailing aloud beside her dead husband, King Brahmadatta came up and offered his love to her. Canda looked at the king and shouted, "How could you think that I would forgive the man who killed my dear husband?" The king was impressed with Canda's devotion and prayed to the gods for help. Sakka, the king of gods, appeared and restored the Bodhisattva's life.

16 The Gnat and the Bull

A gnat was buzzing around a bull. Eventually he settled on the beast's horn. Feeling guilty, he said to the bull, "Sorry to have disturbed you, sir. But I couldn't really help it. If you think it's my weight that is troubling you, don't hesitate to tell me. I will move out of the place and find some other place to sit on." The bull heard this and was amused very much. He said, "Don't trouble your mind for that my friend. I am not bothered about you. I don't feel your weight. Rather I did not notice you at all. It is only after hearing your voice I came to know you are sitting on my horns. Stay there or go. I don't care."

165

17 The Man with Two Wives

A middle-aged man had two wives. One of them was young and vibrant, while the other one was elderly, reserved and a bit conservative. The young wife wanted her husband to look younger than what he was. So she used to pluck the grey hair from his head every day. On the other hand, the other wife preferred her husband to look his own age. Vying with the young wife, she would pluck the black hair from her husband's head every day. The man was happy to have equal attention from his two wives. But one fine morning he found, to his utter dismay, that there was no hair in his head at all.

If you get influenced by conflicting choices, you often end up having no choice at all.

18 The Ass, the Cock and the Lion

Long ago an ass and a cock used to live together in a farmyard. One day a lion was about to pounce on the poor animal when the cock saw what was happening and crowed loudly. The lion took fright at the sudden noise and chose to take to his heels. The ass, noticing the lion running away, was much amused. He thought it would fetch him great honour if he chased the king of forest. So he ran after the lion, but suddenly the beast turned and pounced on him. The ass lost his life then and there. Presumption begins in ignorance and ends in ruin.

19 The Travellers and the Hatchet

Two friends were walking along a road when they suddenly found a hatchet lying under a nearby bush. "Oh! Look what I have found!" one of them exclaimed.

His friend replied, "Don't say 'I', say 'we'. As a matter of fact, we both have found the hatchet."

As they argued, the man to whom the hatchet belonged came searching in their direction. The moment he saw them holding his hatchet, he cried, "Thieves! So you are the ones who took my hatchet." As the two friends stood quietly, the man repeatedly started accusing them of stealing.

The one who had first found the hatchet said to the other, "Alas, we are now done for."

This time his friend said, "Don't say 'we', say 'I am done for."

Those who do not share their fortunes have no right to share their troubles either.

20 The Old Man and Death

An old man was walking a long distance with a heavy bundle of sticks. He was tired and soon collapsed to the ground. He threw his bundle of sticks away, saying, "O Death, please come and take me away. I am old and tired and cannot carry on any more."

Death heard his prayers and appeared before him in the form of a dark somber figure. "I am Death. Were you calling me? Do you want me to take you along with me?" he asked.

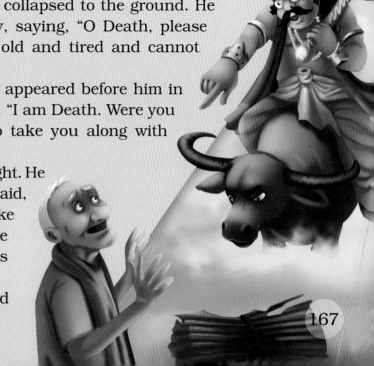

The old man was awed at his sight. He started stammering in fear, and said, "No-no, sir! I do not want you to take my life. I just called you to help me pick up the bundle of sticks that is lying there on the ground."

It is one thing to call death and another to actually die.

21 The Three Tradesmen

Once upon a time, three tradesmen lived in a city. One day, their city was preparing to meet an impending attack from the neighbouring state. The three traders were worried and started planning how to defend their city. One of them, who was a dealer of bricks, said, "Friends, bricks are the best way to fortify a city. Even cannonballs cannot penetrate the resistance put up by a strong brick wall." Another tradesman, who was a dealer of wood, suggested that timber was the best solution and offered his own argument. The third tradesman, who sold leather, said, "Friends, all said and done, I must say there is nothing in the world to defend a city like leather."

Every man for his trade.

22 The Boy and the Bottle

There once lived a little boy who loved the hazel nuts and berries that his mother used to give him every day. One day, the little boy wanted some more nuts, and he put his hand into a bottle containing them. He grabbed a handful and tried to pull his hand out. But the neck of the bottle was too narrow and his hand got stuck. The little boy burst into tears as he struggled in vain to free his hand. A wise friend came up and offered a suggestion. "Don't attempt to take too much at a go, dear boy," said the friend. "Hold half of the nuts in your hand and let the other portion go. Once your hand comes out, you can take a second chance and get the rest."

23 The Thief's Mother

One day a boy stole a book from his schoolmate and brought it home. Instead of rebuking him, his mother encouraged him to get more good things the same way. He grew up, but his childhood habit stayed, and he kept stealing things. One day he was caught red-handed and sentenced to death. When he was being taken to the gallows, his mother was standing in the crowd and wailing for her son. The son came up to his mother and said, "Stop crying, Mother! I am suffering today only because of you. You did not punish me when I stole my schoolmate's book. Instead you encouraged me to be what I am today. If you had corrected me when I was young, I would never have had to face this day."

Evil should be nipped at the bud.

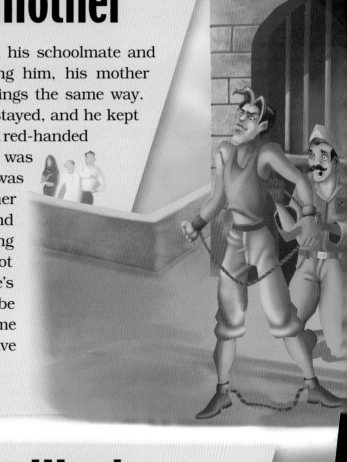

24 The Boy Who Went Swimming

There lived a fun-loving boy who was interested in all kinds of sport. One day he went swimming so far out in the river that he could not struggle against the strong current. As the boy began to sink, he caught sight of a man standing on the shore at a distance. He yelled to him with all his might and asked for help. But instead of coming to the boy's rescue, the man stood there and started advising the boy that he should be more careful in future. The boy was gasping for breath and was desperate. He said, "O please, sir, save your sermon for later. Do something practical and save me now."

Advice without practical help is of no use to anyone.

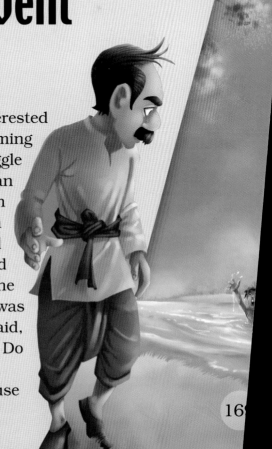

25 The Astronomer

Once there lived a very observant astronomer who would watch the stars with such keen interest that he used to forget everything around. He used to roam the city and watch the stars from various spots. One day he failed to notice an open well and fell into it. He was scared and helpless and began to cry. A passer-by stopped and saw the astronomer struggling to get out. He listened to the poor man's pleas, chuckled and said, "O dear friend! You are always trying to solve the mysteries of the heavens above. But it is not right to ignore the common objects near your feet. You deserve to suffer."

Indifference towards ordinary things often leads to danger.

26 The Boastful Traveller

A globetrotter lived in a village and spent most of his time boasting about the many heroic things he did in the different places that he had visited. The villagers listened but hardly believed all that he said. One day he said that when he was in a place called Rhodes, he had leaped such a distance that no man could ever leap any farther. One of his listeners said, "That sounds great, friend. But there is no witness. Let's suppose this is Rhodes. Now leap and prove that you can really accomplish the feat. We are all watching." The globetrotter sat silent and shamefaced.

The best way to cure a boaster is to

27 The Eagle, the Cat, and the Wild Sow

An eagle made her nest at the top of a tall tree. A cat came to live in a hole in the trunk and a sow lived at the foot of the tree. The cat was very cunning and wanted to drive away the eagle and pig families.

She said to the eagle, "The sow is going to dig up the roots of this tree! When we fall down with our families, she will eat us up."

The eagle was scared and stopped flying out to look for food. The cat next went to the sow and said, "The eagle wants to eat your little pigs. You must never leave them alone!"

Now even the sow was scared and stopped going out for food.

Soon the eagle and the pig family died of hunger, leaving not only the whole tree for the cat but also became food for the sly cat and her kittens.

28 The Moon and Her Cloak

One day the moon said to her mother, "Mother, please make a cloak for me. It must fit me well." Her mother replied, "How can I make a cloak for you? It's impossible." The moon was annoyed. "Why? I too feel like dressing up sometimes," she cried.

Her mother replied, "Yes, my child. But your case is completely different."

The moon asked, "Why is that so?"

Her mother said, "See, right now you are small and in the new moon stage. You will go on to become a bigger full moon, and in the coming days, you will neither be completely big nor small. No gown in the world can ever fit you well."

171

29 The Sun's Marriage

It was a hot summer day when all the creatures of the earth got to hear a rumour that the sun was soon going to tie the nuptial knot. They were all beside themselves with joy. The frogs too were overjoyed and celebrated the happy news with umpteen leaps in the water. An old toad came up with a serious face and reminded them that it was an occasion of sorrow rather than of joy, "My friends! Why are you so happy? Is the news really something we should be celebrating? A single sun scorches us with such blazing heat. Think of the time when there will be a dozen kids of the sun. Our plight on the earth will become more than double, and we may not survive

30 The Ass's Shadow

A man hired an ass with a driver for a long journey on a hot summer day. After travelling some distance, he dismounted from the ass and lay down to rest in its shadow. The driver of the ass, however, got angry at this.

"Sir," he said, "I can't allow you to take sole advantage of my ass. I have as much right to rest in its shadow as you."

"How on earth can you make such a claim?" the man shot back. "I will enjoy this privilege alone, as I have hired the ass and it belongs to me for the entire day."

"No," said the driver. "You hired the ass, but not the shadow. I'll not let you enjoy it no matter what you say." As they quarreled on, the ass took to its heels and ran away.

Quarreling about shadows, we often lose sight of the substance.

1 The Price of Greed

The king of Benaras had a very clever minister who always gave the king sound advice. Pleased with his service, the king decided to appoint him the headman of a village responsible for collecting taxes. The minister gladly went to the village where he was warmly welcomed by the villagers.

The villagers held their headman in great esteem. They completely trusted his decisions and followed his advice without raising a question. However, he was a greedy man and wanted to hoard as much wealth as he could through his collections. So he made friends with some bandits and struck a wicked deal with them. "I'll take the villagers to the jungle on some pretext, and when they are away, you can enter the village and rob the houses. But remember, you will have to give me half of the loot," the headman said.

So a day was decided upon, and the headman led the villagers to the nearby jungle saying they needed to hunt some deer for the village feast. Without the least idea of any foul play, the villagers gleefully accompanied him, singing merrily on the way.

Meanwhile, the robbers entered the village, robbed all the valuables and also took away the cattle. On the same day, a merchant from a distant land happened to come to trade in that village. When he saw the empty houses, he decided to wait on the outskirts till the villagers returned. As he stood waiting, he caught sight of the bandits running away with goods and cattle. He also saw that the headman was leading the villagers back to the village, asking them to beat their drums loud so as to chase away any wild animals close by. But it was just another of his tricks to caution the bandits of the returning villagers.

When the villagers reached the village, they were shocked to see that all their belongings had gone. "What will we do now? We've been ruined," they lamented.

Pretending to be very sad and concerned, the headman said, "This is indeed a serious wrong done to us. We have to find the culprit and punish him."

Just then the merchant, who had witnessed everything, walked up and announced loudly, "This headman of

yours is a cheat. He's the one who helped the bandits run away with your valuables by asking you to beat the drums while returning from the jungle. He has joined hands with the bandits." The angry villagers reported the matter to the king. On investigation, the headman was found guilty. The king said to the headman, "You will not only be given rigorous punishment, but your honoured title, privileges and luxuries will be taken away. Your greed has cost you a lot."

With this, he sentenced the greedy headman to life imprisonment and gave each villager a hundred gold coins and a cow as compensation for their loss.

2 The Trumpeter Taken to Prison

A trumpeter was once jailed as a war prisoner. When he was arrested and taken to the jail, he cried to the guards, "O sir, please leave me. I did not kill a single person. I just accompanied them with my instruments. I inspired them to move forward and fight hard. That was all I did."

The guards smiled at his request. They said, "But my friend, we think you should be punished for the very reason. You never took part in the mass killing. But you always provoked others to kill others mercilessly. You are more crooked by profession than the soldiers who kill and die in the war. He who stirs others to indulge in homicide and bloodshed is certainly worse than the killers themselves."

3 The Farmer and the Fox

There was once a fox, who always troubled a farmer by eating up his hens from the poultry farm. The farmer was really fed up and decided to teach the fox a lesson. After many days, he finally caught the fox.

In his anger, he picked up a length of rope and soaked it with oil. He then tied the rope to the fox' tail and set it on fire.

But it was not only the fox that was harmed. The fox ran into the farmer's crops with its burning tail. Soon all the crops caught fire and were destroyed! If only the farmer had not acted out of anger, he would not have had to suffer such a big loss. He was very sorry to have lost his temper and vowed never to act out of anger again.

4 King Bharu

Long ago there were two groups of ascetics. One group lived under a banyan tree towards the north of the city of Bharu, whereas the other lived under a tree towards the south. After a very cold winter, the tree in the south withered away leaving the ascetics homeless. Wandering here and there in search of a new home, they reached the tree in the north and tried to drive away the ascetics who were staying there. This led to a quarrel between the two groups, whereupon the king was asked to solve the matter. The ascetics from the south bribed him and turned the judgment in their favour. Enraged at this injustice, the gods sent a terrible storm that submerged the whole city under the sea. Everyone died, except only the good people.

5 Love and Kindness

Once upon a time, the king of Varanasi held a grand festival. Many kings attended it. The nagas and the garudas also took part in the celebrations.

Amidst all the revelry, a naga laid his hand on the shoulder of the person sitting next to him without noticing that he was a garuda. Now, garudas and nagas happened to be age-old enemies and the former always maintained an upper hand over the other. So, when the naga realized his mistake, he ran for his life, and the garuda followed him in hot pursuit. The naga saw an ascetic meditating beside his hermitage and went and hid behind him. The garuda, out of respect for the old man, gave up the chase so as not to hurt the holy man.

The ascetic, who knew the two were sworn enemies, spoke to them soothingly and taught them the value of love and kindness. The naga and the garuda shook hands and were friends.

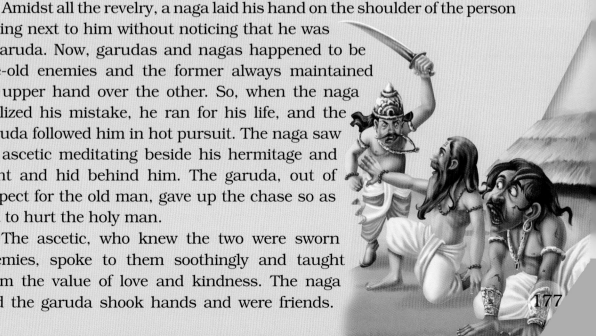

177

6 The Prince and the Brahmin

The Bodhisattva was once born as Junha, the son of King Brahmadatta of Benaras. One day, while walking down a road, he ran into a poor brahmin and scattered all his alms. Feeling sorry for the damage, he said to the brahmin, "Sir, I am very sorry to have caused you so much loss. I have nothing with me that I can give you now. But I promise to compensate you handsomely once I am a king. Please remind me when I ascend the throne."

A few years later, Junha became the king of Benaras. One day, when he was travelling through the city, the brahmin came in front of his chariot and cried, "Long live the king!" Then he went on to ask for what Junha had promised him. Junha remembered instantly and showered him profuscly with gifts.

7 The Wind and the Sun

One day the sun and the wind had an argument as to who was stronger than the other. Finally the two decided to test their powers. They said that the one who could make a man take off his clothes would be the winner. The wind started blowing on a fully-clad man walking along the street. As it blew harder on him, the man wrapped his robe more tightly around his body. The wind hit him with all his might, but the man fought back and managed to save his clothes. Next, it was the turn of the sun. It started shinning in full glory sending brightness and warmth all around. The man felt hotter and hotter and took off his clothes one by one until he was almost next to naked. The sun thus won the contest.

Persuasion is more powerful than physical force.

8 The woman and the Sheep

Once upon a time, there was a woman who had a pet sheep. In order to get wool, she used to shear him so closely that sometimes the scissors would cut his skin. It was extremely painful for the sheep, and he often felt that he might die during the shearing.

One day, as the old woman was busy cutting his wool, he cried out, "O my mistress, why are you torturing me in this way? Will my blood add any value to the wool you take from me? If you need my flesh, send me to a butcher. If you want my fleece, send me to a shearer who will properly clip my wool and not my flesh."

Cutting small costs may cause great damages.

9 The Virtuous Man

The Bodhisattva was known to all as a famous teacher. One day a man came to him with a unique problem. He had four beautiful and virtuous daughters who were all in the marriageable age, but he did not know what quality to look for in the prospective grooms, beauty, nature, nobility or virtue.

Learning about all the qualities of the suitors, the Bodhisattva said, "Handsome features will wither with time; experience is what anyone can gather gradually; noble lineage does not ensure that the man will be noble. But virtuousness is the only quality that really endures. A man's virtues remain on the earth even after his death, as a person is always remembered for his good deeds."

Hearing this, the brahmin married off all of his four daughters to a virtuous man.

10 The Woodcutter

A woodcutter was once cutting down the large trees by a river. As he hacked at the thick trunks, his axe slipped from his hands and dropped into the river. The woodcutter sat down and started sobbing.

After some time, Mercury, the god of the river, appeared with a shining golden axe in his hand. The woodcutter said, "No, sir, that is not the axe I am weeping for."

Mercury then showed him a silver axe. The woodcutter said, "Sorry, sir, this is not mine either." Mercury smiled and lifted up a third axe. This time it was the one that the woodcutter had lost. The woodcutter was overjoyed. "Yes, this is the one that I owned," he cried.

Mercury was highly pleased with his honesty and gifted him all the three axes.

Honesty brings rewards.

11 Traitors Must Accept Treachery

A fox and an ass were good friends. One day they decided to go hunting together. They were roaming the forest when they suddenly saw a lion at a distance. They realized that it was too late to turn and run and that they had to find some other means of escape. With a trembling heart, the fox went up to the lion and tried to negotiate with him. "If you promise to spare me, I can fool the ass and bring him to you," he whispered.

The lion seemed extremely pleased, and, patting his back, he declared, "Well said, my boy. I like your plan." The fox soon brought the ass to the lion and the latter killed him instantly. Just after he had finished making a good meal of his flesh, the lion jumped on the fox and killed him for his next meal too.

Treachery never pays.

12 The Lump of Gold

Once, while ploughing a plot of land, a poor farmer found a huge lump of gold under the soil.

"Good Lord! Who has buried such a precious thing in the field," the farmer wondered. Thinking it unsafe to carry it in broad daylight, the farmer buried it again and returned in the night to take it home. But it was too heavy for him. He tried dragging it with ropes, but that too proved to be of no use. Then the farmer tried to think of some other solution.

After much pondering, he said to himself, "I'll divide the lump into four parts and carry one part at a time." So he broke the gold into four pieces of equal size and took them home one by one. From that day on, the farmer became a rich man.

13 The Power of Generosity

Once a rich man became famous for his charitable acts. He lived next to a poor hermit called the Silent Buddha. The hermit was an enlightened person who spent all his time in meditation. One day he went to the rich man to beg for food. Mara, the god of death, was jealous of the rich man's reputation and decided to stop him from giving alms. When the rich man came forward to offer food to the Silent Buddha, Mara gave rise to a huge fire between the two. But the rich man was determined to comfort the hermit. Trusting the strength of his good deeds, he walked through the fire and offered the Silent Buddha food. Mara felt ashamed and went away, saying, "Indeed the power of generosity is great."

181

14 The Merchant, the Ascetic and the Ram

The Bodhisattva was once born into a family of merchants. One day he saw an arrogant ascetic clad in a leather garment. The man put up the bearing of a saint and asked everyone around to bow to him and show respect. After a while, the Bodhisattva noticed that a ram was lowering his head in front of the ascetic. The ascetic took it to be an expression of respect for him and was highly pleased. But the Bodhisattva knew that the ram was getting ready to attack. Apparently the ram didn't like the leather garment the ascetic was wearing. The Bodhisattva ran up and tried to warn him. But before the ascetic could hear anything, the ram knocked him down. All his pride was shattered as he lay groaning on the ground.

15 The Straw Worth More Than Gold

A crafty ascetic lived as a guest in a rich man's house. One day the rich man buried all his gold coins in the ascetic's room. The ascetic pretended not to have seen. When the man left, he dug up the gold coins and hid them under a tree outside. Next day, the ascetic took his leave from the rich man. After a while, however, he returned with a straw and handed it to the rich man, saying that he would not take anything with him that did not belong to him. The Bodhisattva, who lived nearby as a merchant, saw this and sensed foul play. He asked the rich man to check if his gold coins were safe. The theft was soon discovered, and the Bodhisattva said that the ascetic must be the culprit. He was caught and made to return the coins.

16 The Eagle and the Tortoise

A tortoise once thought it would have been better if he could fly on the sky. Seeing the birds, he fancied so many things about life. He called an eagle and offered him the treasures of the sea.

"In exchange," he said, "you have to teach me the art of flying."

The eagle said, "My friend, it will be dangerous for you." But the tortoise didn't listen to the eagle. So, the eagle was forced to take him to the sky. And after reaching a considerable height, he said to the tortoise, "stretch your legs and get ready. Now fly," and he left him there. The tortoise, before he could utter a single word, fell down from the sky and smashed his head against a rock.

17 Two Ambitious Princes

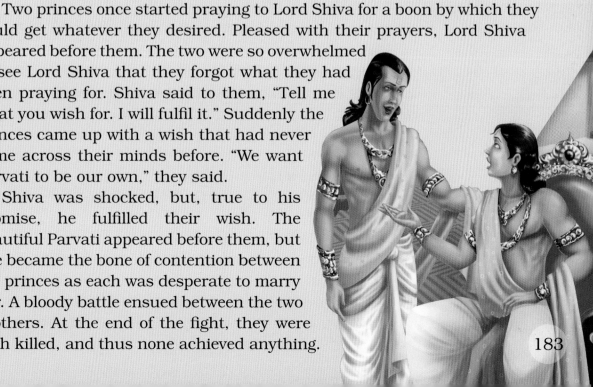

Two princes once started praying to Lord Shiva for a boon by which they could get whatever they desired. Pleased with their prayers, Lord Shiva appeared before them. The two were so overwhelmed to see Lord Shiva that they forgot what they had been praying for. Shiva said to them, "Tell me what you wish for. I will fulfil it." Suddenly the princes came up with a wish that had never come across their minds before. "We want Parvati to be our own," they said.

Shiva was shocked, but, true to his promise, he fulfilled their wish. The beautiful Parvati appeared before them, but she became the bone of contention between the princes as each was desperate to marry her. A bloody battle ensued between the two brothers. At the end of the fight, they were both killed, and thus none achieved anything.

183

18 Prince Five-Weapons and Sticky-Hair

A royal couple had a son whom they named Five-Weapons. When he grew up, they sent him to the best of teachers for education. After his schooling was over, Five-Weapons started for the palace. On the way, he passed through a forest that was inhabited by a dreadful monster called Sticky-Hair. Sticky-Hair challenged Five-Weapons to a fight. But every weapon that the prince used got stuck in the monster's hair which was sticky and matted. Finally, the prince himself got stuck to the monster's hair. But the prince did not lose courage. Instead he thought of a way to fool the monster. "Inside my belly, there's a weapon made of diamond which will cut through and kill you as soon as you devour me," he said to the monster. Scared, Sticky-Hair set the prince free. Thus the prince saved himself by the strength of his intelligence.

19 The Sacrifice of Vessantara

A man called Vessantara was famous for his sacrifices. Among the many animals that he owned, there was a white elephant named Pacchaya who had the supernatural power to evoke the Rain God. Vessantara donated this elephant to the king of Kalinga when the latter's kingdom was facing drought. One day a brahmin named Jujaka visited Vessantara and begged to have his two sons. Vessantara was heartbroken, but he gave them away to the brahmin. Hearing of Vessantara's sacrifice, Sakka, the king of gods, decided to test Vessantara's generosity. He disguised himself as a beggar, came to his house and begged for his wife. This time too Vessantara agreed, although he was deeply grieved to part with her. Sakka was impressed with his magnanimity and revealed his true identity. With his blessings, Vessantara got back everything he had sacrificed.

20 Two Merchants and the Sacred Tree

Two merchants, Wise and Verywise, made a huge profit and decided to share it. Verywise demanded twice the amount of Wise's share, arguing that his very name justified it. The two merchants went to a sacred tree to seek its advice. Verywise asked his father to hide in the hollow trunk of the tree and pretend to be its spirit. When the two merchants put forward their arguments to the tree, Verywise's father said from inside it, "Verywise deserves a double share of the profit for he is the wiser one." Sensing foul play, Wise set the tree on fire.

Out came Verywise's father, crying, "God save my poor soul. It's better to be a loser than a cheat."

21 Brahmadutt and the Crab

A man named Brahmadutt had to visit a faraway city. His mother gave him a small crab in a box, saying, "This crab will be your companion on the journey."

"How can this mute little creature be a companion to me?" he asked. But he set out on his journey holding the box.

After some time, he decided to rest under a tree. He put the box down and fell asleep when a snake slipped out of a hole in the tree. Just then the crab escaped from the box and killed the snake with its sharp claws.

When Brahmadutt woke up, he found a dead snake lying near. He realized the crab had saved his life.

22 Demon in the Desert

Two friends, Sridhar and Shanidhar, were rich merchants. One day they decided to go to a distant land to trade. On the way, they had to cross a desert which was the territory of a huge demon, a fact unknown to the two friends. Sridhar, the more adventurous of the two, opted to go first, thinking he would enjoy the journey better. Shanidhar agreed and let Sridhar go first, thinking he would have a safer journey. On the way, Sridhar and his men lost their way in the dreary waterless land. The demon, disguised as a traveller, misled them and ate them all up. Some months later, Shanidhar started his journey. But he was wise enough to see through the demon's disguise and guard his men and himself against his evil tricks. They reached their destination, finished their business and returned home safely.

23 The Happy Man

One day a sage and his chief disciple were busy discussing some religious issues when the king of the land arrived there to pay homage to the sage. The chief disciple was so absorbed in his conversation with the sage that he failed to notice the king approaching.

The king heard him saying, "O, what a pleasure! What a pleasure!"

He felt contempt for the disciple and loathed his fawning attitude. The sage, however, read the king's mind and told him about the disciple's true identity. He explained that the disciple once used to be a monarch but had renounced everything for the life of a recluse. The "pleasure" the king had heard him talking about was actually his happiness in being an ascetic. The king realized his mistake and apologized immediately.

24 The Belly and the Other Organs

Once upon a time all the limbs and other organs of the human body rebelled against the belly. The belly used to lead a lazy life and they decided to cut the supply line to belly. The hand said, "I will no more lift a single morsel of food." The mouth said, "I will not chew anything."

The leg too decided not to carry the belly from this place to that place. Slowly the whole human body came to a state of inertia. Lack of food resulted in weakness and sickness. They all started suffering together. Then one day they understood that the limbs and the organs of the human body are interconnected. The belly is an integral part of the body. So they started cooperating with it as ever to stay alive healthily.

25 Great Gift and the Wish-Fulfilling Gem

The Bodhisattva was once born as a kind-hearted prince named Great Gift. One day the prince went to a nearby village and saw the sufferings of his poor subjects. Moved with pity, he offered them riches. But it wasn't enough to rid everybody's poverty. So he decided to get for them the Wish-fulfilling Gem that lay in a fountain on Jewel Island. He set out on a long voyage and finally reached the island. But the inhabitants did not welcome the prince who was little more than a stranger to them. But Prince Great Gift did not lose heart. He helped the king of the island to strengthen the defenses of the castle where the Wish-fulfilling Gem was kept. Pleased with his goodness and services, the king gifted him the gem and the prince took it home. It brought everyone enough riches to fulfil their needs.

26 The Truth about the Two Bags

There is an old saying that a man is born with two bags. One bag hangs from his neck on his breast and the other on his back. The two bags are full of faults. The one in front carries the faults of his neighbours. The one on his back is full of his own faults. The truth of this funny saying is that man is never able to see his own faults but always notices the faults of others. He is perpetually blind to his own drawbacks and is always critical about what others do.

27 Poison Dice

Once upon a time there lived two gamblers. One of them was good at heart whereas the other was dishonest. Whenever the latter sensed that he was losing a gamble, he used to furtively swallow the dice and exclaim that it had got lost. Once, noticing the trick, the other gambler vowed to teach him a lesson. Next day, he smeared the dice with poison before the game started. After a while, when the dishonest man began to lose, he sneaked the dice into his mouth as usual. Immediately the poison took effect and he fell sick. But the other gambler, a kind person, nursed him back to health. "My friend, I did this just to teach you a lesson. Never ever deceive a friend," he said.

28 The Selfless Prince

One day a man came up to a certain king and, introducing himself as the former prince of a neighbouring state, asked for a job.

The king kept him as his bodyguard. That night, the king heard a woman sobbing and sent the prince to check the matter. In reply to the prince's queries, the woman said, "I'm Goddess Laxmi. I am crying because I have to leave this place."

The prince said, "O great goddess, our master will be in grave trouble if you leave. How can we make you stay?"

The goddess said, "You have to make a sacrifice of your son." The prince agreed, unaware that the king was watching him. The prince went ahead and sacrificed his son, his wife and even his own life to appease the goddess and stop her from leaving.

The king rushed to the temple and said to the goddess, "Mother, the prince is a virtuous man. Please bring him and his family back to life."

The goddess was moved and fulfilled the king's wish.

29 The Conqueror of Anger

The Bodhisattva, the enlightened being, renounced all worldly pleasures to lead an ascetic's life. His beautiful wife too resolved to be with him in his new life of abstinence. Together, they built a hut in a forest and started staying there. One day the king of the land saw the Bodhisattva's wife, fell in love and decided to kidnap her. To test the Bodhisattva's powers, the king came to him and asked him what he would do if a thief or a wild animal attacked his wife. The Bodhisattva said, "I would not be angry." The king laughed at this and pulled the Bodhisattva's wife into his chariot. But the Bodhisattva remained calm. The king was surprised and asked why he showed no anger. "Anger is man's greatest enemy," replied the Bodhisattva. It destroys his inner beauty and leads him away from the path of happiness." The king was impressed with his greatness, begged for forgiveness and released his wife.

30 The Ass and the Lion

An ass and a lion lived together in a cave. One day they decided to go hunting. They roamed the whole forest but found no creature they could catch. When they returned, they found some goats inside their cave. The lion asked the ass to go inside and drive away the goats while he would wait outside and kill them one by one as they came out. The ass was very excited with the plan. He went inside and started kicking, braying and making such a fuss that not only the goats but even the lion got confused. But the plan worked, and the goats were killed by the lion as they ran out one after the other. When all was over, the ass asked the lion how he had liked his wonderful performance. The lion said, "You would have scared me away too, had I not known you are an ass."

31 Heart of Gold

Once there lived a benevolent rich man who used to help every needy person who came to his door. Because of his exceptional generosity, he was known to all as "Heart of Gold." One day, the gods in heaven decided to test the strength of his generosity by putting him in a state where he would have nothing to give away. So they disguised themselves as a band of thieves, went to the rich man's place and robbed him of his entire wealth. After some time, God Sakka dressed himself as a beggar, went to the rich man and begged for food. The rich man was eating the only piece of bread he had left, but he gave it to the beggar. Impressed with his kindness, the gods blessed him and returned all his property.

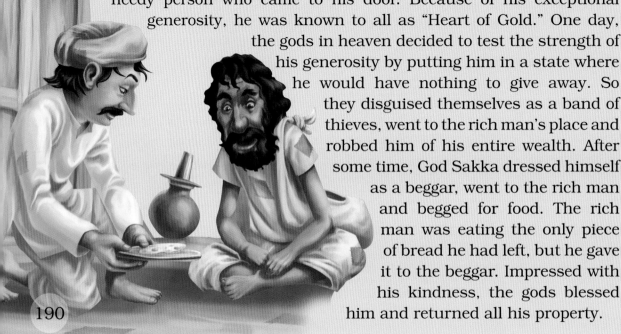

1 The Unlucky Weaver

Somilaka was an expert weaver who could make the finest garments fit for kings and princes. But he was very poor, and so he decided to try his luck at another place called Vardhamanapuram. Working day and night, he managed to make three hundred gold coins within three years. He decided to return now and started on his homeward journey. At dusk, he found himself in the middle of a forest. He climbed a tall tree and went to sleep on a high branch. In his dream, he saw the god of action and the god of destiny talking to each other.

The god of destiny asked the god of action, "This weaver is not destined to live in luxury. Why did you give him three hundred coins?"

The latter replied, "I have to give what they deserve to those who toil hard. Whether the weaver can keep it or not is in your hands."

The dream jolted the weaver awake. He looked into his bag and found his coins missing. Heartbroken, Somilaka began crying, "I cannot go home and face my wife a penniless man." He decided to go to Vardhamanapuram and try to earn money again.

This time, he made five hundred gold coins in one year. This time too he had

the same dream. He immediately looked into his bag and found there was no gold in it.

Somilaka lost all hope and decided he would commit suicide. Suddenly he heard a voice in the skies: "O Somilaka! I am Destiny, the one who took away your wealth. But I am pleased with your hard work and sincerity. Ask for a boon, and I shall grant it."

"Please give me lots of wealth," said the weaver.

"In that case, go back to Vardhamanapuram where you will find two wealthy merchants, Guptadhana and Upabhuktadhana. Study them well and decide who you want to be: Guptadhana, the man who earns a lot but does not spend a cent, or Upabhuktadhana, the man who earns but also enjoys his wealth."

Somilaka followed the advice and went back to Vardhamanapuram.

He went to Guptadhana's house and asked to stay for the night. Guptadhana agreed but grudgingly gave dinner to Somilaka, suggesting that he was an unwanted guest. The next day, Guptadhana had an attack of cholera and had to miss his meal. So it turned out that what he had given away to Somilaka was saved.

Later, Somilaka visited Upabhuktadhana's house. Here he was welcomed in with great love and respect. The weaver had a good meal and slept soundly. The next day, a messenger from the royal palace came to Upabhuktadhana and gave him a big sum of money on behalf of the king.

Somilaka thought to himself, "It is better to be like Upabhuktadhana. He enjoys life with whatever he has. What's the use of being rich but miserly?"

Pleased with his choice, the gods showered wealth on him.

2 The Sandy Road

One day, a merchant decided to go to the town to try his fortune. He arranged for some men who could go along with him. They had to cross a desert to reach the town.

When they reached the desert, it was very hot. So, the merchant and his people waited for the night to resume their journey. As the night fell, they resumed their journey. One of them had some knowledge of the stars. So, he was guiding the way to other people by reading the position of stars. They travelled for the whole night without taking any break. At daybreak, they stopped and camped.

After travelling for two days, they found that it was just one more day's journey, after which they would arrive at the town. Suddenly, they found that there was no water left with them. Every one was tired and had no energy left to continue travelling without water. So they sat down. The merchant decided to find water. He walked down.

Finally, he saw some grass and thought, "There must be water somewhere below, otherwise, that grass would not be there."

All of them ran with the merchant and started digging.

The merchant jumped down into the hole they had dug and kept his ear to the rock. He called to them, "I can hear water running under this rock. We must not give up." Then, the merchant came out of the hole and said to the serving boy, "My boy, if you give up, we are lost. Please go down and try."

The boy stood up raising the hammer high above his head and hit the rock with his full strength. He didn't give up, thinking the words of the merchant. Ultimately, the rock broke and the hole was full of water. All the men drank water, as if they could never get enough. They watered the oxen and took bath.

After drinking and bathing, they split the extra wooden yokes and axles from their carts. They made a fire out of it and cooked their rice. They had their meal and rested through the day. They also placed a flag on the well, so that the passing travellers could see and have water. After the sunset, they started their journey and reached the town in the morning. They sold the goods making huge profits and happily returned back to their village.

Will and Determination can achieve anything.

3 The Honest Potter

An honest potter met with an accident which left his forehead scarred permanently.

Days passed, and there was a famine in the village. The potter was jobless, and so he left his village and went to another land. There he got recruited in the king's army. One day, the king arranged a mock battle to test the strength of his army. He came across the potter and, seeing the deep mark on his forehead, said to himself, "He must be a brave warrior."

"In which battle did you get this deep injury?" asked the king.

The potter replied politely, "Sir, I used to be a potter. I never fought a battle in my life."

The king got angry. "Soldiers, here is a liar. Punish him," ordered he.

The potter cried, "O sir, I am not a warrior but I have a good physique fit for combat. Moreover sir, I could have lied to you, but I chose to take the risk and told you the truth. There is no reason why you should punish me."

The king was pleased with his frankness and awarded him a handful of gold coins.

4 The Story of Mittavanda

A famous teacher of Benaras had a very disobedient student named Mittavanda. All he did during classes was eating and fighting with other students.

His behaviour went from bad to worse. The teacher finally asked Mittavanda to leave his school. Mittavanda decided to leave the place all together. He went to a small village and settled down as a labourer. He also married a poor local woman and had two sons. As time passed, the villagers learnt that he had been a student of a famous teacher. They started coming to seek his advice whenever they were in trouble.

But things did not turn out well for Mittavanda. The villagers soon found that ever since they started taking Mittavanda's advice, their troubles increased. They all felt he must be a mischievous man, and they got together and drove him away.

5 The Fearless Ascetic

A young sage was travelling with a caravan of merchants. The caravan halted for the night, and everyone lay down to sleep. But the sage remained awake and kept pacing up and down near the tents. Suddenly he saw some robbers surrounding the caravan.

The ascetic prepared himself for attack. Using a long stick, he started a lone and fierce fight against the robbers. "Cowards! You can't even beat one person. What will happen if I call my brothers?" asked the ascetic as he swung his stick around.

The robbers were taken aback with his amazing strength and courage and they soon fled.

Next morning, when the merchants found out what had happened, they thanked the sage profusely. "Weren't you scared of the robbers?" they asked.

The ascetic smiled and said, "The sight of robbers causes fear to those who are rich. I am penniless. Why should I be afraid?"

6 The Green Wood Gatherer

One day some students went into the woods to gather firewood. One of the students noticed a tree which had no leaves. He dozed off below it, thinking he would be able to break a few branches easily and get back in time. In the evening, he woke up and found that the branches above were actually green and not too fit for firewood. But the student was late, and so he took home some of the green branches. Next morning, the cook used the same to make breakfast for the students. But it took a long time to light the fire, and the students got delayed for an important journey to a remote village. When the teacher got to know the reason for the delay, he said wisely, "Don't put off for tomorrow what you can do today. A lazy person who does so puts others into trouble."

7 The Golden Swan

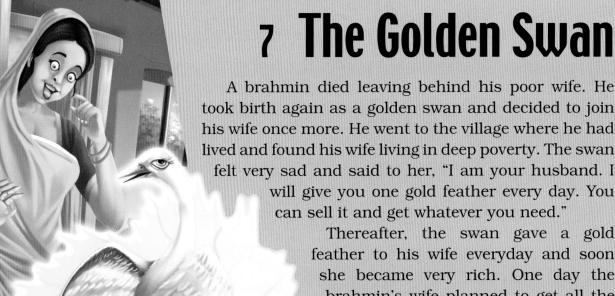

A brahmin died leaving behind his poor wife. He took birth again as a golden swan and decided to join his wife once more. He went to the village where he had lived and found his wife living in deep poverty. The swan felt very sad and said to her, "I am your husband. I will give you one gold feather every day. You can sell it and get whatever you need."

Thereafter, the swan gave a gold feather to his wife everyday and soon she became very rich. One day the brahmin's wife planned to get all the gold feathers at once. So she caught the swan by his throat and tried to pluck all his feathers.

The swan struggled free and flew away forever. Thus the greedy woman lost her future earnings.

8 The Disobedient Son

A merchant had a disobedient, irreligious son. Intending to rouse his interest in religion, his mother sent him to listen to a saint's sermons in the temple; she promised to give him a thousand rupees if he attended the whole session. The greedy son at once agreed. But instead of listening to the saint's teachings, he slept during the entire session.

Next morning, the son came home, took a thousand rupees from his mother and started making plans for moving overseas to trade. His mother pleaded with him not to go, but the man refused to listen to her. He packed his things and left for the voyage. But alas! His ship met with a terrible storm on the way, sinking all passengers on board.

Thus the son paid the price of disobedience.

9 A Man Named Curse

Anathapindika had a friend named Curse. While Anathapindika lived a prosperous life, Curse was an unsuccessful man. Anathapindika put him in charge of his finances. Curse began to stay in Anathapindika's house.

But Anathapindika's relatives were not happy with Curse's presence as he had an inauspicious name. Some time later, when Curse was alone in the house, some robbers sneaked in. Curse was alert and quickly thought out a plan. He created a lot of noise in a way as if he was waking up everyone. The robbers got confused and left the house.

When Anathapindika returned, he got to know about the incident. He thanked Curse and told his relatives they had a wrong notion about Curse. "There is no harm in a name. I am sure everyone will learn a lesson from this incident and try to get rid of superstitions," he said.

10 A Fair Price

There was a king who had a dishonest young treasurer. Once he gave a merchant only a cup of rice in exchange for his herd of horses. The merchant was very annoyed.

The next day he went to the royal court and said to the king, "O Lord! I want to know the real value of one cup of rice." The king asked the treasurer to answer the merchant's question. The treasurer wanted to please the merchant and said, "Sir, a cup of rice is worth the whole kingdom of Benaras."

The king was aghast and realized his mistake in appointing the young man as his treasurer. He made a new deal with the merchant for his herd of horses and banished the treasurer from his kingdom.

11 The Story of Matanga

In the olden times, a man called Matanga belonged to a so-called low caste. One day, on his way home, he chanced upon Ditthamangalika, a beautiful maiden, and her friends. The maidens, who were of a higher caste, considered it unlucky to even see a low-caste man, and so they beat up Matanga.

Matanga felt humiliated and decided to fight against the evils of the caste system. He began a hunger strike outside Ditthamangalika's house, demanding her hand in marriage. For seven days, he did not eat or drink anything.

Fearing Matanga would die in front of her house, Ditthimangalika agreed to the marriage. "I'm a human being of flesh and blood, just like you. No one has the right to despise me," Matanga told Ditthamangalika once they were married. Ditthimangalika realized her mistake and began to love and respect Matanga. Together, they spread the message of brotherhood and equality.

12 The Power of Faith

One day a lay disciple of the Buddha was returning from the village to the monastery. On the way, he had to cross a river. There was no ferry available at that time. The disciple, reluctant to miss his teacher's evening sermon, started walking through the river.

Engrossed in thoughts of the Buddha, he hardly noticed the level of the water. Suddenly he came to his senses when the water had reached up to his neck. He shouted out in fear," My God! I'm standing in the middle of the river!" He once again closed his eyes and thought about the Buddha's teachings. He managed to walk across to the opposite bank. Thus his faith helped him to reach his destination.

13 Sutasoma

Prince Sutasoma was studying under a sage when a ferocious cannibal named Kalmasapasada abducted him. Sutasoma was distressed because he wasn't able to offer anything to the sage in exchange for his education.

Hearing the prince express his regret, Kalmasapasada took him back to the ascetic. After having laid his offerings before the sage, the prince returned to his captor. Surprised at his return, Kalmasapasada said, "You're truthful but not wise."

The prince smiled and said, "I am wise enough to know that falsehood leads to eternal suffering."

Impressed with the prince's words, Kalmasapasada offered to release him, but the prince said, "How can you set me free when you yourself are a slave to your own cruel instincts?"

His words stirred the cannibal's heart, and he started leading a virtuous life.

14 The Robber and the Courtesan

The Bodhisattva, who once lived the life of a robber, was caught and sentenced to death by the king of the land. While he was being led to the execution site, Sama, the chief courtesan of the city, saw him and fell head over heels in love.

She sent word to the governor that the prisoner was her brother and that she would give him a thousand gold coins if he set the Bodhisattva free for a while. She then persuaded a youth, who was madly in love with her, to take the place of the prisoner. So the Bodhisattva was released and the youth was executed in his place. The robber, though happy to be free, couldn't trust Sama. "If she can kill her innocent admirer for another man, then she might kill me for someone else once she gets tired of me," thought he. So he went away leaving Sama in despair.

15 Asadisa, the Skilled Archer

The Bodhisattva was once born as Asadisa, the elder son of the king of Benaras. When he grew up, he became a skilled archer. When his father was dying, he made his younger brother the king because he felt his elder son Asidasa was not interested in the throne. Asidasa, however, was miffed. He left the kingdom and became an archer in the army of a neighbouring king.

One day the kings of seven neighbouring states attacked Benaras together. Asidasa went and barged into the tent where the seven kings were having their dinner and, with one miraculous shot from his arrow, broke all the seven plates in which they were having their food. He announced that they had to stop the battle or else he would kill them all. Terrified, the kings immediately retreated.

Asidasa's younger brother, the new ruler of Benaras, rushed to the scene. He thanked and welcomed Asidasa, and asked him to take up the throne. But Asidasa declined.

16 A Wise Teacher

Once there lived a prince named Gamani. He had a very wise teacher who advised him on all his political affairs. Prince Gamani always followed his teacher and soon became very popular among the people. After the king's death, the people happily made Gamani their king.

This angered the other princes. They threatened war against Gamani if he didn't relinquish his power. Following his wise teacher's advice, Gamani declared in the presence of his brothers that he would divide the royal wealth among all of them. Hearing this, the princes thought that the portion each of them would get would be too small and that if they waged war for the throne, the whole kingdom would be divided into small portions all the same. So together they decided to accept Gamani as the king.

17 The Boy Who Cried Wolf

Long ago, there was a shepherd boy who used to take his flock of sheep to the forest. One day, he decided to play a trick on the villagers. He shouted, "Help! Wolf!"

The villagers heard his cries and came rushing. When they reached the boy, they saw there was no wolf around. The shepherd boy laughed loudly at them. He played the same trick on a few more occasions, so the villagers began to doubt his cries.

It so happened that one day, a wolf actually came. The shepherd boy ran towards the village, shouting, "Help! Wolf!"

The villagers thought that the boy was up to his old trick again. "A wolf is attacking my sheep. Please help me," he cried desperately.

But the villagers laughed at him. As the boy kept pleading, the villagers reluctantly went to the spot. But by the time they reached there, they found that the wolf had killed many of the boy's sheep.

18 The Miserly Father

A sixteen-year-old boy, Mattakundali, came down with severe jaundice, but his father was reluctant to spend money on a physician. He tried to treat the boy on his own, but the boy's condition grew worse.

The Buddha saw the poor boy and was moved. He came and sat at the dying boy's bedside and recited beautiful religious sermons. The boy, in his last moments, felt deep faith in the Buddha's teachings. The boy died and, from then on, his bereaved father would go to the funeral ground and weep pitiably sitting by his son's ashes. Seeing this, Sakka, the king of gods, appeared before him and admonished him for his miserliness that had caused the death. The repentant father then gave up grieving and started following the teachings of the Buddha to make up for his sins.

19 The Old Woman's Hut

Vikramaditya, a kind and just king, decided to build a palace on the riverbank. But near the palace site, there stood the hut of an old woman. The king met the old woman and offered to buy her hut at any price she asked for.

The old woman said to the king, "This hut is dearer to me than my life. I have lived all my life in it and I want to die in it. It is the only memory of my late husband."

The king thought for a while and then said, "Let people see my palace and her hut standing side by side. They will appreciate my taste for beauty and my love for justice."

20 The Wine Bottle

One day an old woman found an empty wine bottle lying on the floor of an old house. The bottle was sending out a sweet fragrance of good liquor, and the old woman picked it up eagerly. But it was totally empty; not even a drop remained at the bottom. The old woman removed the cork of the empty bottle and pressed it to her nose. Inhaling deep, she exclaimed, "Wow, I wish I could have seen you when you were full! How beautiful you must have been that you still smell so good. Your beauty has outlasted the ravages of time."

Memories outlast our transient pleasures.

21 The Water-Sprite and the Princes

Three princes felt thirsty while roaming in a jungle. The eldest prince asked his youngest brother to fetch some water from the nearby river. In the river, there lived a water-sprite who used to cast a spell on anyone who could not give the right answer to her question, "What are good fairies like?" The youngest couldn't answer her question, so the water-sprite carried him away into her cave. The same thing happened with the second prince when he came to fetch water.

As none of his brothers returned, the eldest prince got worried and went to look for them. The water-sprite appeared and asked him the same question.

"Good fairies never harm innocent souls," replied he. The answer pleased the water-sprite extremely, and she returned him both his brothers.

205

22 The What Not Tree

A merchant, along with his caravan, was once travelling through the forest. They stopped for the night under a tree loaded with fruits. The merchant recognized it to be the poisonous What Not tree and warned his men not to pluck any fruits from it.

But the fruits looked ripe and delicious, and some of his servants greedily plucked and ate them. The poisoned fruits killed them immediately.

Next morning, everyone wondered how the rest of the servants had escaped the temptation of the What Not tree. "We could make out the danger from the unusual fact that so many ripe fruits were hanging from the tree without being touched," the surviving servants replied. Everybody, including the merchant, appreciated their intelligence.

23 The Mulla Pleads Poverty

Mulla Nasruddin once borrowed a large sum of money from a moneylender and failed to return it on time. The moneylender went to court, and the Mulla was brought before the judge.

Faced with trial, the Mulla admitted to have borrowed a hundred gold coins and promised to return it even if he had to sell his cow or horse. Hearing him, the moneylender shouted out, "My Lord, he's lying. He doesn't have even have food in his house to feed his family, leave alone owning animals."

At this, the Mulla said wittily, "My Lord, if he knows that I'm so poor, doesn't he know that I am not in a position to return his money immediately?" The judge accepted the Mulla's argument and dismissed the case.

24 Sakka Plans to Tempt Noble Kassapa

Once the Bodhisattva was born as Kassapa, the son of a royal chaplain. Kassapa and the prince were childhood friends and pupils of the same teacher. When the prince ascended the throne, Kassapa became an ascetic and acquired supernatural power through meditation. Sakka, the king of the gods, became scared of his growing power and decided to curb it. One night, Sakka appeared in front of the king and asked him to persuade Kassapa into killing animals. "Do what I say, and one day you'll rule over the whole world," said Sakka. The king agreed and sent for Kassapa, but the latter had already learned about the plan and refused to meet him. Thus neither a god nor a king was able to dissuade the Bodhisattva from his own way of life.

25 The King Who Knew the Language of Animals

Once, a king saved the life of a serpent. The pleased serpent in turn gifted him the power to understand the language of animals provided he kept it a secret. If he revealed the secret he would have to die.

One day, when he was sitting with his queen in the garden, he heard an ant speak about a piece of sweet and he smiled as he listened. The queen pressed him to tell her the reason of his smile despite the king explaining to her the consequences. The king was about to reveal his secret. Suddenly, a heavenly voice said, "O king, why should you sacrifice your life for someone who doesn't value yours?"

The king then accused his wife of being selfish. The queen realized her mistake.

207

26 The Brahmin Who Lost His Spell

Once upon a time a young brahmin learned a magic spell from a wise chandala. By this charm the brahmin could grow delicious mangoes even out of season. Once, during winter, he made delicious mangoes grow in the royal garden in front of the king.

The amazed king wanted to know who taught him the spell. The brahmin was reluctant to acknowledge his humble teacher, and so he said that he had learned the skill from a brahmin in the city of Takkasila. But as soon as he said this, all his magic power deserted him. This shamed the youth, and, at the king's orders, he went to his teacher to ask for forgiveness. The teacher was deeply hurt, but he forgave the brahmin.

27 The Stupid Son

There lived a carpenter who had a shiny bald head. One day the carpenter was sawing wood to make a bed when a mosquito caught sight of his shiny head. "Let me sit on this bald head and enjoy a sumptuous meal," he thought and flew down on it.

When the mosquito started biting, the carpenter felt irritated and tried to chase it away with his hand. Though the mosquito flew away, it was reluctant to leave and kept coming back. The carpenter then called his son and asked him to help him get rid of the mosquito. "Don't worry, Father. I'll kill him with one blow," said the son and hit hard with his hand. The mosquito was killed, but alas, the carpenter's head received a mighty knock!

28 The Ungrateful Husband

A prince and his wife, while returning from a long journey, felt very hungry. Some hunters passing by gave them a roasted rabbit to eat.

But while his wife was away fetching water, the prince ate the whole rabbit. When she came back, he said that the rabbit had run away leaving only its tail in his hand.

Later, the prince became the king, but he did not give his wife her due honour as the queen. The Bodhisattva, who happened to be the king's minister, saw the injustice and reminded the king how he had wronged her before. The king realized that he had been unfair to his dutiful wife for long and gave her the status she deserved.

29 The Two Pots

Two pots, one made of clay and the other made of brass, were swept into a river current. As they were tumbling down the stream, the brass pot said to the clay pot, "Friend, come closer to me. I'll protect you or you'll drown." The clay pot said, "Thanks, my friend. I know you have a noble heart with a good intent, but still I would like to stay at a distance from you. If you collide with me in the force of the current, I'll turn into pieces and you'll stay unharmed. So it is better we keep away from each other."

It is wise to keep your distance from a neighbour who is much stronger than you.

30 The Elephant and the Pack of Jackals

A pack of jackals saw an elephant and wanted to make him their food. One old jackal said, "Here I can show you the way. I will in a way kill him."

The elephant was roaming here and there when he met the old jackal. "Sir, I am a jackal. I have come as the representative of all other animals. We had a meeting and we concluded that we should have a king here. You have all the qualities of a king in you. So please follow me, we'll be grateful if you take the charge."

The elephant was very flattered to hear this. He followed the jackal. The jackal took him to a lake where the elephant slipped and got stuck in thick mud.

"Help me my friend." shouted the elephant helplessly. The jackal smirked viciously and said, "Sir you trusted someone like me. Now you must pay for it with your life."

The elephant kept stuck there and as time past by, he died. The jackals had a great feast of his flesh.

1 The Foolish Sage and the Cheat

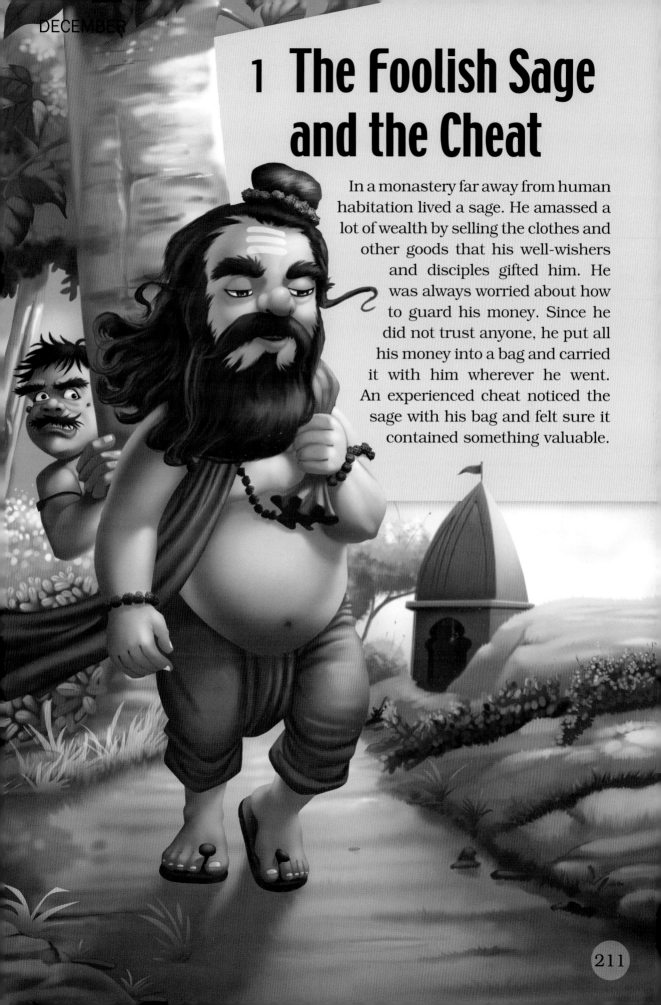

In a monastery far away from human habitation lived a sage. He amassed a lot of wealth by selling the clothes and other goods that his well-wishers and disciples gifted him. He was always worried about how to guard his money. Since he did not trust anyone, he put all his money into a bag and carried it with him wherever he went. An experienced cheat noticed the sage with his bag and felt sure it contained something valuable.

He began planning a way to steal it from him.

The cheat approached the sage, fell on his feet and said, "O wise one, please show me the path that will deliver me from all worldly ties."

Pleased with his humility, the sage said, "Child, I shall accept you as my disciple, but you must not come into my hermitage to stay because company is forbidden for a sage. After initiation, you have to live in the hut at the entrance of the monastery."

The cheat promised the sage that he would consider every sign from him as a command and carry it out word for word. He began making the sage happy by attending to every need of his.

But the cheat was not able to carry out his plan. The sage never set the bag anywhere out of his sight. The cheat thought to himself, "The old man is very crafty. Shall I kill him and take the bag?"

One day a disciple came and invited

the sage to his village to perform the sacred thread ceremony for his son. The sage accepted the invitation and set out for the village, taking the cheat with him.

On the way, the guru and his disciple had to cross a river. After bathing in the river, the sage took the money bag, pushed it beneath a quilt he was carrying and told the disciple, "I have to respond to nature's call. I am leaving this holy quilt here. Keep an eye on it." The moment the guru went out of his sight, the cheat took the bag and fled.

Meanwhile the sage, who trusted his disciple, joined a crowd of people watching two well-fed goats fighting ferociously. A jackal came there to feast on the blood the two goats were shedding. The sage saw the jackal entering the scene and thought it would surely get caught between the two warring goats and die. His guess came true, and the jackal was soon gored to death by the two goats.

Brooding over the demise of the jackal, the sage returned to where he had left his disciple and panicked when he found him missing. The holy quilt was there, but the bag in it was missing. He began wailing, "Oh, you trickster! What have you done? I have lost everything in this world now." After a vain search for the cheat, the foolish sage returned home dejected.

2 A Tale of Two Friends

In a city, there lived two friends named Dharmabuddhi and Papabuddhi.

Cunning Papabuddhi planned to deprive Dharmabuddhi of all his wealth. He told Dharmabuddhi, "Dear friend, I strongly feel it is not safe to keep all our wealth at home. We should bury our money in some secret place in a forest. Whenever we need money, we can go there and get it."

Dharmabuddhi agreed, and they dug a pit deep inside a nearby forest and buried their earnings in it. One night Papabuddhi went to the pit and stole all the money. Next morning, he went to Dharmabuddhi and asked him to accompany him to the forest because he needed money.

When both of them arrived at the pit and found it empty, Papabuddhi began shouting loudly, "Dharmabuddhi, you stole the money. You must give me half of what was buried here." Though Dharmabuddhi denied it vehemently, Papabuddhi persisted in his accusations.

The case was brought to the court. There Papabuddhi said to the judge, "I can produce the gods of the forest as witnesses. They will determine who is guilty." The judges agreed and asked both parties to be present the next morning at the forest.

Papabuddhi went home and told his father, "Father, I have stolen all of Dharmabuddhi's money. There is a court case going on, and I can win it only with your help. Go now and hide in the hollow of the big tree in the forest. Tomorrow morning, when the judges and others assemble there, I will ask you for the truth. Then you say that Dharmabuddhi is the thief."

The father hesitated to lend support to the wicked plan, but finally he agreed as he loved his son.

The next day, while Dharmabuddhi and the judges watched, Papabuddhi went near the tree and shouted, "O gods of the forest, you are all witnesses. Declare who among us is guilty."

The father shouted back from inside the hollow of the tree, "It is Dharmabuddhi who stole the money."

Dharmabuddhi felt suspicious. He filled the tree hollow with hay, poured oil on it and threw a matchstick in. The fire forced the father to come out of the tree.

"All this is the work of Papabuddhi's evil mind," said the father to the judges. The king's men arrested Papabuddhi.

3 The Farmer and the Sea

A ship carrying sailors was being tossed about in a furious storm. A farmer, watching from the shore, cried out, "O sea! Your appearance is so deceptive. You look placid and calm, and people are tempted to sail on you. But when they do so, you change your mood and kill them mercilessly. You are really unfair."

The sea heard his words and replied in a woman's voice, "O farmer! It's not me who caused the storm today but the wind. When the tempestuous gusts fall on me, my waters cannot remain at rest. The sailors are victims of the wind, not me. Without the wind, I am a mild and gentlc being."

4 The Fox without a Tail

A fox once survived the attack of hunters, but he lost his tail. Feeling ashamed of his appearance, he decided to do something to save his face. He called a meeting of the foxes and said, "I have had a revelation, my worthy brothers, and I have got rid of my tail by divine instruction. I am leading a happy and easy life now. Our tails are ugly and burdensome. Strange that we do not clip them by our own will. I suggest you follow me and cut down your tails too."

A sly fox stood up, chuckled and said, "Had I lost my tail, I would have found your proposal very convincing. But I still have it, and I see no reason why I or anyone else should cut it. We must avoid suggestions given out of selfishness."

216

5 The Crow and the Pitcher

It was a hot summer day, and a crow was feeling very thirsty. Looking all around for water, he saw a pitcher, flew up and peeped inside. But the pitcher was empty except for a little water at the very bottom. The crow knew he had to overturn the pitcher or break it, but he did not have the strength to do either. However, he did not lose hope and looked around to find something that could solve the problem. He found a heap of pebbles lying close to the pitcher, and it gave him an idea. The crow carried the pebbles one by one and dropped them into the pitcher. As the pebbles piled up inside, the water level rose and gradually reached the brim. The crow drank to his satisfaction. Necessity is the mother of invention.

6 The Comedian and the Farmer

A comedian, while performing in a competition, mimicked the sound of a pig. People liked it and clapped for the performer. Suddenly, a farmer shouted out, "What's so special about the act? I can do it too."

The farmer was allowed a chance on the stage. He had a small pig hidden under his shirt, and he stealthily tweaked the ear of the pig until it squealed loudly as he stood on the stage. But the crowd wanted to see the comedian as the winner of the competition. They started shouting that the comedian was far better in his imitation of a pig. The farmer was furious. He took out the pig from under his shirt and showed it to the audience. "See. You prefer the imitation to the real thing."

7 The Fisherman and the Hunter

A hunter was coming down the mountains loaded with game. Suddenly, he came across a fisherman carrying a bag full of fish. The two met and, in a few minutes' conversation, became friends.

The fisherman longed to eat game, and the hunter expressed his desire to have a dinner of fish. So they happily exchanged their stuff. They soon made it a habit of meeting and exchanging their catch every day. One day, while they were eating together, a wise man came up. He noticed the exchange, thought for a while and then said, "My friends, if you keep on doing this on a regular basis, soon you will lose the pleasure of sharing and tend to keep what you have got. Pleasure is best attained through abstinence."

8 Monster Becomes Human

A prince once met a monster in a jungle, who wanted to eat him up. The prince was not in the least frightened. Instead, he said, "You are very mighty indeed, but you lack intellectual power." The monster was taken aback. He calmed down and requested the prince to teach him how to be intellectually powerful. The prince asked him to first change himself into a human being.

The monster reduced himself to a common man's size and stood humbly before the prince. They lived together in the forest till the prince imparted all his knowledge to the monster. He named the monster Vineet.

When the teaching was over, the prince prepared to bid him farewell. But Vineet requested him to take him along. The prince happily agreed, and together they proceeded to the palace where they lived happily ever after.

9 Four Friends

Three friends, a rat, a tortoise and a crow, lived in a jungle. One day, they met a deer, who was running as if scared. On being asked, the deer said, "The king's men will come here tomorrow for hunting. I'm running for my life."

Hearing this, the rat, the tortoise and the crow also ran to save their lives. On their way, the tortoise was caught by a hunter. The rest hit on a plan to free him.

The deer lay still on the road as if he was dead and the crow pecked his body.

When the hunter saw this, he put his bag down and went up to the deer. As he was busy inspecting the deer, the rat helped the tortoise free himself and get out of the bag. The deer too jumped up and sprinted away far out of the reach of the hunter.

Their unity gifted them their freedom.

10 The Dog and His Master

A man was getting ready for a long journey. It took him hours to pack his clothes and other necessities, and he soon felt tired and exhausted. He looked at the cumbersome pile of luggage and sat down for a moment or two to take a breath. He saw his pet dog standing still near the door and gaping at him. He scolded the animal, saying, "What are you doing there, you lazy laggard? Go and get ready as soon as possible. Don't waste time." The dog listened to his master and calmly said, "Master, I am always ready. I do not need to take anything along. It's you who is spending time in packing up so many things."

219

11 The Oak and the Reeds

An oak tree was once uprooted by a vicious storm. It lay flat on the swamp for days when one morning it was astonished to see that a slew of reeds had grown on its trunk. The oak was overwhelmed with emotion, and said to the reeds, "This is so strange! I used to be a firm and robust being with the strength to fight the strongest wind. But I failed and got uprooted. You are a weak and fragile lot, and it's easy to nip you in the bud. Then how come you have survived the storm and flourished so well?"

The reeds smiled and said, "It's not that amazing, is it? You were destroyed in fighting against the storm, while we survived by yielding and bending to the slightest breath that was blown."

12 The Countryman and His City Wife

There was a famous teacher in Varanasi. One of his students from the countryside fell in love with a girl from Varanasi and married her.

But, after his marriage, the student became irregular in his classes. On one occasion, he appeared after a long absence, and the teacher wanted to know why he had kept away. The student heaved a sigh and confessed, "Guruji, my wife's behaviour is troubling me a lot. One day she behaves very well, but the next day, she becomes rude. I am too distressed to attend classes."

The teacher consoled his student, saying, "Some people are born with an unpredictable nature. Accept her the way she is."

The student followed his advice and never got upset by his wife's behaviour again. After a while, his wife, too, realized her mistake and mended her ways.

13 The Geese and the Cranes

Some geese and cranes were feeding together in a field when a bird-catcher suddenly appeared and tried to catch them. The cranes, being lighter and quicker, escaped his clutches and flew away to a safer distance. But the heavy geese could not move fast and tried to escape the bird-catcher by hopping all around the place. They soon fell into the net and the bird catcher took them away.

When in danger, it is better to be light and smart than heavy and slow.

14 The Doctor and his Patient

A doctor was once treating a young critically ill patient, but he failed in his efforts and the patient eventually died. While attending his funeral, the doctor said, "I am so sorry that he died at such a tender age. If only he had desisted from drinking and smoking, he would have lived longer. He had a good constitution, but he has wasted his life with his bad habits."

The mourners came up to the doctor and said, "Sir, all your wisdom is useless now. Why did you not warn him when he was alive? None of us wanted him to die so young. Your advice has come too late."

15 The Vain Jackdaw

Lord Indra once decided to make a king among birds. He asked all the birds to come to him on a certain day so that he may crown the most beautiful one. The jackdaw knew he was very ugly. So, he went around the jungle, collecting feathers of other beautiful birds. He stuck these onto his body and became the most beautiful of all. When the appointed day arrived, and the birds had assembled before Lord Indra, the jackdaw also came looking fine and colourful. Lord Indra liked his many colours and decided to make him the king. But all the birds angrily protested, and they plucked off their own feathers from the jackdaw, who once again became ugly. You can never hide who you truly are, so its best to be yourself.

16 The Prince and the Hermit

There was a cruel king whom people called Kroor Singh. One day he was stuck in a storm and took shelter with a hermit. A parrot, a rat and a snake also took shelter in the hermit's cottage. At night the hermit served food to his animals first and then to the king. This made the king very angry, but he chose to remain quiet.

The storm subsided, and the king left with the promise that he would always help the hermit in return for the favour. One day the hermit went to the king to ask for help. The cruel king remembered his experience on the stormy night and ordered his servants to kill him.

The hermit told the soldiers all that had happened, and the soldiers were so enraged that they killed the king and declared the hermit their new ruler. The new king brought over the snake, the rat and the parrot to the palace, and they all happily lived together.

17 Buried Treasure

An old man buried all his earnings deep inside the forest as he didn't want it to fall into the wrong hands. His servant, Nanda, was the only one who knew about it. After his death, Nanda promised to help his master's son find his inheritance. He took the boy to the forest, but suddenly he became hostile and refused to cooperate.

Later there were many occasions when Nanda agreed to help, but each time he backtracked after reaching the forest. Puzzled at his behaviour, the son went to a wise man for advice. The wise man said, "Your treasure lies at the spot where Nanda changes his mind and turns back. It is only when he comes near his little area of power that he turns back on you."

Next time, when they went to the forest, the son dug up the place where Nanda stood and turned and he finally found the wealth.

18 The Man and the Satyr

A satyr and a man became friends and were walking down the road on a cold wintry day. The man held the palms of his hands to his mouth and blew into them. The satyr asked the man why he did so. The man said, "I am warming my hands."

The satyr and the man started staying together. A few days later, they were sitting and dining together when the man began blowing at his bowl of porridge. The satyr was amazed to see this. He asked him, "Why are you blowing into your porridge?"

The man said, "It's too hot. I am trying to cool it."

The satyr was confused and said, "My friend, we cannot stay together any longer. It is not safe for me to stay friends with someone who blows hot at one moment and cold on the next."

19 The Silkworm and the Spider

There once lived a spider and a silkworm who were both skilled weavers. The spider was arrogant and very proud of his webs.

One day, he said to the silkworm that he was more skilled than the silkworm. He challenged the silkworm.

"Let us have a weaving competition and see who is better!"

The silkworm agreed. The spider worked rapidly and soon completed the web.

"Just look at it," he said, "How grand and delicate it is."

After a while the silkworm too finished producing the softest, finest yarn of silk.

Just then a princess walked by with her friends. She saw the spider web and angrily asked for it to be brushed away. Then she saw the silk yarn and exclaimed in delight, "Oh! Collect that fine silk yarn my friends, I will have it made into my royal robe."

Something designed to trap and kill, even though it may be beautiful, will never be appreciated as art.

20 The King with One Grey Hair

Long time ago, the Bodhisattva was born as King Makhadeva. When the king was almost eighty-four years of age, his royal barber spotted a grey strand of hair on his head and pointed it out. King Makhadeva realized he was growing old and regretted having squandered all his years in worldly pleasures. He went ahead, renounced all his powers and anointed his eldest son as the new king. When his subjects heard about it, they rushed to him. "Oh dear king, why do you want to leave us?" they cried.

The king smiled and said, "My dear subjects, God has sent the message that death is nearing. All my life, I thought about wealth and power, but now is the time when I should seek my salvation in prayer and meditation."

21 Lord Vishwakarma and the Camel

A camel went to Lord Vishwakarma, the creator of all things, and requested him to grant him two horns. "Lord, I feel defenseless at times. The ox has horns, the boar its tusks, the lion its claws, but I have nothing to protect me. I should be given two horns at least so that I can fight back if someone tries to attack me."

Lord Vishwakarma became angry at his demand. "If you look carefully at yourself, you'll find yourself endowed with unique qualities. Don't think of other animals. Stay content with whatever you have," he said, and twisted the camel's ears as a token of punishment.

You should be content with you have.

22 Interdependence

One day the trees in a forest were having a heated discussion.

"All animals come to rest in our shade and dirty the place when they leave," said one tree.

"We must teach them a lesson," cried another.

So, one day, when the animals gathered there, the trees swayed so violently that they ran away in fear. The trees felt happy to get rid of the animals.

However, they soon realized their mistake when the next day two woodcutters approached the trees with their axes. One of them said to the other, "Finally, the animals have stopped coming here. We can now peacefully cut the trees for wood." They started chopping up one of the trees while the surrounding trees watched helplessly.

225

23 The Unwelcome Guests

A rich businessman lived in the city of Ujjain. He had four sons-in-law, who arrived one day as his guests.

The businessman became concerned as they showed no signs of going back. The businessman then asked his wife not to give their sons-in-law water to wash their feet.

One son-in-law, who was very intelligent, understood that they were no longer welcome. So, he left immediately.

The next day, the three remaining sons-in-law were given very shabby chairs to sit on. The second son-in-law too departed for his home. The third son-in-law too left for his home after he was served stale food.

But the fourth son-in-law refused to take all the unwelcome hints that his in-laws gave him. Finally, the businessman forced him out of the door.

24 The Red Bud Tree

Once the eldest prince of a land went into the forest in early spring to see the Red Bud tree. The tree was bare, and the prince could not understand why it was called Red Bud.

Later in that season, his younger brother went there and saw that the tree was covered with beautiful red buds. The third brother went next, and this time it was full of green leaves.

Sometime later, the youngest prince went there and saw that the tree was full of green pods.

The four brothers had an argument about the actual nature of the tree, as each one had seen it looking different. The king, who had overheard their argument, came forward and explained to his sons that each of them had seen the same tree in different stages of its life.

25 The Brawny Ox

A man called Jeevan had an extremely strong ox. One day he threw a challenge to the villagers, saying, "I will prove that my ox can pull a hundred wagons at a time in a row. If I fail, I will give away a thousand silver coins. If I win, you will have to give me the same amount."

Some rich persons accepted his challenge.

The next day the ox was brought forth, and the villagers were all surprised to see his huge brawny appearance. They arranged for a hundred wagons all joined together in a row, and the ox was soon harnessed to the first one.

Jeevan whipped his ox and cried, "Start fast, you devil!" The ox had never been abused by his master, and he refused to budge. In spite of all his coaxing, Jeevan failed to move him even the slightest bit. He soon realized his mistake and said sorry to the ox. The satisfied animal then pulled the row of wagons, and Jeevan won the challenge.

26 Hanuman and the Charioteer

A charioteer was carelessly driving his chariot along a muddy road. Suddenly his wheel got stuck in deep mud and the horses came to a standstill.

The charioteer started lamenting and without making any effort to get out of the trouble, he started calling Lord Hanuman, when he appeared before him and asked, "What do you want?" "I am in deep trouble; please help me pull my chariot out of the mud."

Lord Hanuman was annoyed watching him only praying and not trying his bit. He said, "Try to help yourself. God helps him who helps himself. Self help is the best help." The charioteer put all his efforts then and managed to drag his chariot out without any help. Hanuman left the place with a smile.

27 An Insightful Guru's Mantra

A sage foresaw some grave misfortune to the king that would come in the form of his own son.

He told the king, "When your son reaches the age of sixteen, some misfortune will fall upon you. Therefore, I will give you a mantra that will save you from any danger."

The prince had a wicked nature. When he reached the age of sixteen, he made a plan to kill his father.

One day the prince waited with his sword while the king was climbing the stairs. While stepping upwards, the king suddenly remembered and recited the sage's mantra. The words of the mantra meant that a king who has a son must be very careful while going up the stairs.

The prince heard the mantra and was stunned. He dropped the evil plan and started living like a good son.

28 The Bats

Once upon a time, there was a huge battle between the beasts and the birds. The bats took part in the war but kept on changing sides. When the beasts were about to win, the bats were found supporting them. But on the next morning, things changed and the birds seemed to be winning. The bats promptly left the beasts and joined the birds. When at last the birds were announced the victors, the bats got busy celebrating the victory. Everyone around, both birds and beasts, were shocked with their behaviour. They got together, openly denounced the bats and expelled them from the animal community. Since then, bats live in dingy holes of trees and come out only after dark. Deceitful creatures deserve to be shunned.

29 Lord Shani and the Sculptor

One day Lord Shani wanted to know what people on the earth thought of him. So he disguised himself as a traveller and entered a sculptor's workshop. There he found statues of various deities. He went up to the sculptor and asked, "Man, how much would you charge for the statue of Brahaspati?"

The man said, "A hundred rupees."

Lord Shani asked, "And how much for the statues of Rahu and Ketu?"

The sculptor named a higher price for those.

Lord Shani looked around and found his own statue there too. Hoping to hear the highest price for it, he asked the sculptor, "And lastly, how much for Shani?"

The sculptor said, "If you pay me for the previous two statues, I'll throw in this statue of Shani for free."

30 Jotipala, the Great Sage

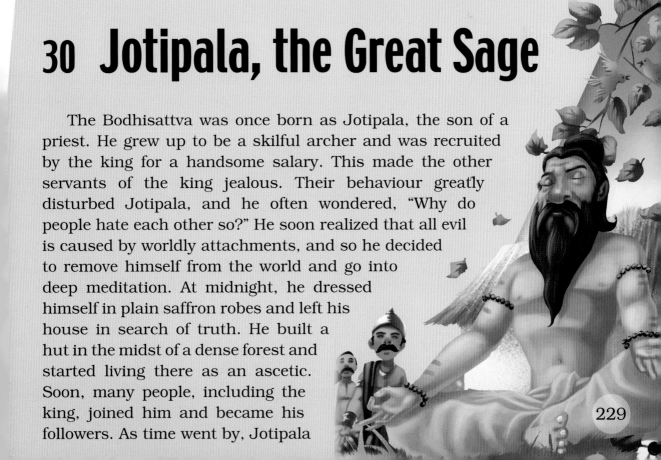

The Bodhisattva was once born as Jotipala, the son of a priest. He grew up to be a skilful archer and was recruited by the king for a handsome salary. This made the other servants of the king jealous. Their behaviour greatly disturbed Jotipala, and he often wondered, "Why do people hate each other so?" He soon realized that all evil is caused by worldly attachments, and so he decided to remove himself from the world and go into deep meditation. At midnight, he dressed himself in plain saffron robes and left his house in search of truth. He built a hut in the midst of a dense forest and started living there as an ascetic. Soon, many people, including the king, joined him and became his followers. As time went by, Jotipala

31 The Clever Astrologer

A king always used to always worry about his death. He would often ask astrologers about his end. One day he called a well-known astrologer and asked him to tell him all details of his life.

First, the astrologer revealed all the positive aspects, which made the king very happy. Then he revealed the negative aspects. This made the king so angry that he asked the astrologer to reveal the day of his own death.

The astrologer understood that whichever day he would predict his own death, the king would disprove the prediction by ordering his death on another day.

So, the astrologer said to the king, "My death will come one day before yours."

That put the king in a fix. Giving death to the astrologer means inviting his own death a day later.

Hc praised the wise forecast of the astrologer and gave him costly gifts.

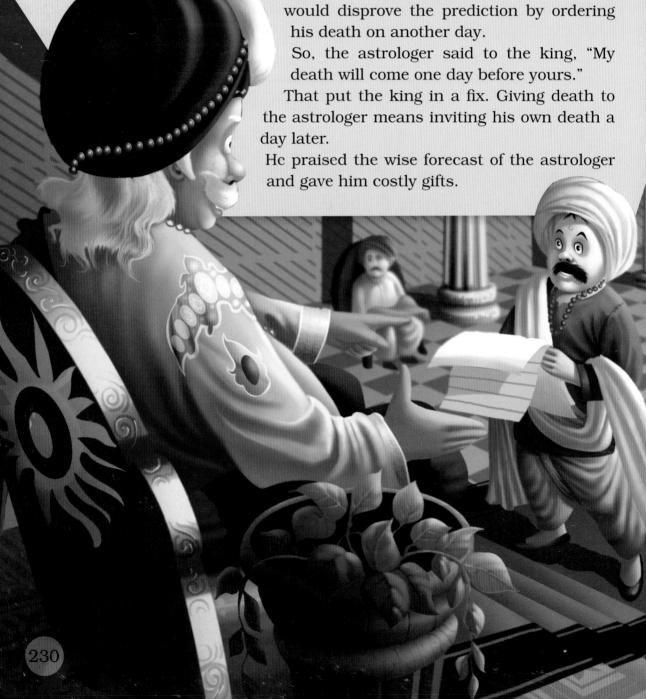